Minute CROSS-WORDS
Tiny Crosswords for Fast Solving

Matt Gaffney

PUZZLE WRIGHT PRESS

New York

CONTENTS

PUZZLE WRIGHT PRESS

New York

An Imprint of Sterling Publishing Co., Inc.
1166 Avenue of the Americas
New York, NY 10036

The puzzles in this book were originally published
in 2014 and 2015 on the website mgdxword.com.

ISBN 978-1-4549-1899-8

Distributed in Canada by Sterling Publishing Co., Inc.
c/o Canadian Manda Group, 664 Annette Street
Toronto, Ontario, Canada M6S 2C8
Distributed in the United Kingdom by GMC Distribution Services
Castle Place, 166 High Street, Lewes, East Sussex, England BN7 1XU

For information about custom editions, special sales, and premium and corporate purchases,
please contact Sterling Special Sales at 800-805-5489 or specialsales@sterlingpublishing.com.

Manufactured in China

2 4 6 8 10 9 7 5 3 1

www.sterlingpublishing.com
www.puzzlewright.com

INTRODUCTION

Everything's smaller these days: cellphones, computers, politicians' brains—you name it. And faster, too, since attention spans are shorter. Why, even this little crossword book introduction has to be snappy or you'll get bored and skip it altogether. Can you imagine the pressure this puts on me?

Newspaper crosswords are traditionally 15×15 squares, since that's what fits nicely on a folded piece of newsprint. But fitting in with modern times, smaller is better—and the puzzles in this book are all just 10×10 squares in size. So instead of spending 15 or 20 minutes with your crossword, these petite puzzles will require only a few minutes of your time.

But that doesn't mean they're not fun. Who needs the standard three or four theme entries when these puzzles get the job done with just two? They might be two entries that resemble each other, like PLAY CATCH and PLAY FETCH, or there might be another connection, like BRONZE AGE and GOLDEN ERA. Sometimes the link may take a few seconds to spot, which adds another little "aha moment."

If you dig these little puzzles, you can find more of them on my website: www.mgdxword.com.

—Matt Gaffney
Staunton, Virginia

ACROSS

1 Jonas who refused to patent his polio vaccine
5 Animals of a given region
10 Oscar-winning role for Whitaker
11 ___ closet
12 "Mansfield Park" novelist
14 Tenochtitlán builder
15 Mineral vein
16 Lock unlocker
17 He surrendered at Appomattox
19 Pizza ___
20 Total jerk
23 Concerning
26 One of the senses
28 "The Maltese Falcon" director
30 Hit half of a record, usually
31 Baseball nickname that reverses to a TV explorer
32 Palindromic pill
33 Daddy

DOWN

1 Seller of vowels
2 Blow away
3 Like laundry room floors, maybe
4 Leg bender
5 Winter hazard
6 Airplane cabin feature
7 Golden rule preposition
8 Have to have
9 Actress Hathaway
13 Rights org.
18 Latin words to a traitor
19 Civic organization?
20 The Jetsons' dog
21 Front steps
22 Fires off an email
23 Cleaner brand that's also a Dutch soccer team
24 Sammy with 609 home runs
25 Slender
27 Right away, in four letters
29 Put a curse on

ACROSS

1 Couldn't get enough of
7 Roadie's equipment
10 Architectural feature
11 Language of southeast Asia
12 "I'll make this perfectly clear ..."
14 Fashion mag
15 Furniture store piece
16 Plagiarizes
17 Inventive Thomas
21 Chemical element from the Greek for "strange"
22 Cake time, for short
26 "Sure, I'll tell you ..."
28 Parks and ___
29 Word before blast or number
30 Yes, at sea
31 Head, in Honduras

DOWN

1 Word in real estate listings
2 Burr-Hamilton, e.g.
3 Australian stone
4 Enjoyed a roller coaster
5 Nightmare street
6 City in Ohio
7 Reason you couldn't have done it
8 Canadian leaf source
9 Sits for the photographer
13 Cat's place
16 Decongestant brand
17 At additional cost
18 "___ Defeats Truman" (infamous headline)
19 How a woolly mammoth may be preserved
20 Scrubbing pad brand
22 "No alcohol provided"
23 Certain noblewoman
24 Neighbor of Calif.
25 Village People song
27 Kingston Trio song

ACROSS

1 Neuters
6 Siestas
10 Georgia city
11 "Now I get it"
12 Bulk, as a purchase
14 T, in Greece
15 Shoot the breeze
16 Radiate
18 Carried on, as a war
22 Used, as a table
24 Symbol of peace
25 Victoria's Secret item
27 Clear choice at the bar
28 Chain for travelers
32 Rooster on the roof
33 "My goodness!"
34 Word on the penny
35 Commission work

DOWN

1 Hits hard
2 Canal land
3 Find not guilty
4 The solver of this crossword
5 Unforeseen problem
6 Respectable
7 Sashimi tuna
8 Vaper's stuff, sometimes
9 It's over your head
13 Slangy refusal
17 iPad, e.g.
19 Words of encouragement
20 Show to be true
21 Build Your Own Grand Slam server
23 One less than tetra-
26 Mall conveniences
28 Shopping station

29 Dubai is there: Abbr.
30 Barack's mother
31 Vote for

ACROSS

1 Insincere talk
5 Wilson of the Beach Boys
10 Cornerless shape
11 Source of songs
12 Safety, in metaphor
14 It's doughy in a deli
15 No problem
16 Down in the dumps
17 "___ be an honor!"
19 Hotel amenity
20 Dickensian outburst
23 Catch a glimpse of
26 Country of Asti spumante wine
28 City that hosted the 1932 and 1980 Winter Olympics
30 See eye to eye
31 Active person
32 Long (for)
33 "___ Karenina"

DOWN

1 Athletic guys
2 Ex of the Donald
3 Legitimate
4 "Desire Under the ___" (Eugene O'Neill play)
5 Sports ___
6 Word before "G" or "PG-13"
7 Concept
8 Voices, as a grievance
9 Prying
13 Indiana Jones's weapon
18 Follow closely
19 Head of cattle
20 Beloved strips
21 Classic sci-fi movie of 1979
22 Many-headed monster of Greek myth

23 Kill, as a dragon
24 Chapter part
25 Slimy vegetable
27 "And there you have it!"
29 Bic writer

1	2	3	4	■	5	6	7	8	9
10				■	11				
12			13						
14				■	15				
16			■	17	18		■	■	
■			19			■	20	21	22
23	24	25		■	26	27			
28			29						
30				■	31				
32				■	33				

ACROSS
1 "Goldberg Variations" composer
5 Feed, as a fire
10 The A of AFK
11 Hosted
12 Valley of vineyards
13 Firing
14 Pervy possession
16 Pigeon's perch
17 Legitimate
22 Propagandize
25 Fail to be
26 Too
27 Terse verse
28 Confessed guilt publicly, maybe
29 Easy as pie
30 Erotic

DOWN
1 The Shins and the Strokes
2 Expect soon
3 "You Can't Take It With You" director
4 Hilton alternative
5 Chiding words before "you"
6 Shout on the street, for those without the app Uber
7 God with a long beard
8 Sweet to people
9 Chang Bunker's twin
15 Get some good laffs in
18 Exchanges
19 Oscar winner Berry
20 Region of southeast England
21 Little ___ (state nickname)
22 Bikini tops
23 Horse controller
24 Paul in an infamous YouTube rant
25 "So that's the deal ..."

ACROSS

1 Like some mobsters
5 Highest room
10 Some are pale
11 Dallas suburb
12 Casual, as remarks
14 Where docs do triage
15 Whistleblower, for short
16 Farmland units
19 Creative inspiration
20 Those people
21 Waste maker
22 It's more in Mexico
23 Bestie
24 Playing golf
29 One of its letters stands for "underwater"
30 "Joanie Loves Chachi" costar
31 Printing goofs
32 Ones who will call you out on your mistakes?

DOWN

1 Dictator with a mole
2 Cat-eater of TV
3 Mos ___
4 Regard highly
5 Mimics
6 A little affection
7 Sign for Chris Brown or David Beckham
8 Pollute
9 Joltin' joe?
13 There are 168 in a wk.
16 Not greater than
17 Unpredictable
18 Prepare for a big day
19 Barbie's beach town
21 Movie computer
23 "Visualize Whirled ___" (mildly humorous bumper sticker)
25 John Oliver's employer
26 "Tropic Thunder" setting
27 "Napoleon Dynamite" dork
28 Morse code plea

ACROSS

1 Stood at home
7 To this point
10 Actor Peter
11 Potential future humans
12 Lame humor, named for a yellow food
14 Murray or Meara
15 "___ we all?"
16 Thin and chic
17 Capital of the Bahamas
21 Creature that always somehow speaks English in sci-fi movies
22 Disc in many desserts
26 Great humor, named for a yellow metal
28 Drill sergeant's syllable
29 Tried again with, as floor tiles
30 Has too much
31 Buildings with tiered seating

DOWN

1 Florida city, informally
2 Loads and loads
3 Not sure which of two options to choose
4 "Don't take that ___ with me!"
5 Ron who was Tarzan
6 That old familiar feeling
7 Unsophisticated type
8 Concert or coronation
9 Preference
13 Settlers of Catan stuff
16 Onetime Supreme Court justice O'Connor
17 "___ Libre" (Jack Black movie)
18 Not just in your head
19 Easily fooled types
20 Get a glimpse
22 Get way more than a glimpse
23 Horse's pattern
24 He directed Marlon to an Oscar
25 Macau calculations
27 "___ So Bad" (Tom Petty song)

ACROSS

1 The jack of clubs and the jack of hearts, say
5 Kind of picture puzzle
10 Hot rod rod
11 Commission earner
12 Special military unit
14 Graffiti, if done well
15 Three letters often not meant literally
16 Arabian boss
19 "You go, ___"
20 Starbucks size
21 Toy truck company
22 Period
23 "The Purloined Letter" author
24 Many members of 12-Across
29 Beck's breakout single
30 Red cup brand
31 Any member of Ace of Base or Roxette
32 Laughing syllables

DOWN

1 Stretch the truth on, as a résumé
2 Swung tool
3 Misfortune
4 Not wholesale
5 Hard-to-steer transportation
6 Inflated view of self
7 City whose wall was infamous
8 Open, as a champagne bottle
9 Brando's bellow
13 Animal rescuer
16 Doesn't pay for
17 1930s bombshell Jean
18 Pass
19 Lighten up
21 Maine toothpaste maker
23 Cut (down)
25 Common contraction
26 Incredible Hulk portrayer Ferrigno
27 Yukon beast
28 Sea plea

1	2	3	4		5	6	7	8	9
10					11				
12				13					
			14				15		
16	17	18				19			
20					21				
22				23					
24			25				26	27	28
29					30				
31					32				

ACROSS

1 Penn of movies
4 Hailed individual
10 Exalting stanzas
11 Watch type
12 Arcade game with barrels and ladders
14 Star sheep
15 Its logo's first letter is red
16 Nairobi native
18 OK for all ages to watch
23 Stage song
27 Bravery
28 Misidentifier of windmills
30 Promise
31 Stir-fry piece
32 Gold, silver, and bronze
33 Not just -er

DOWN

1 Early filmmaker
2 Love so much
3 His tomb is in Red Square
4 Augustus or Julius
5 X number of
6 Oven setting
7 Movie mass, with "The"
8 New York college
9 Like good French toast
13 Most important aspect
17 Ocean forces
19 Luxury ___ (Monopoly square)
20 Forgo a big wedding, maybe
21 Showers attention (on)
22 Awesome
23 Levine or Scott
24 February flower
25 Part of MIT: Abbr.
26 Light blue
29 Net address

ACROSS

1 Rebuffs the affections of
7 No spring chicken
10 With this proclamation
11 Hawaiian paste
12 Famed violinist
14 Zogby or Gallup product
15 Low card
16 Ross Perot and Jerry Jones, for two
17 Refugee's claim
21 Bird or plane
22 Magritte painted one
26 What 12-Across was often seen doing at performances, two ways
28 Frequent blinker
29 Novelist who created Rabbit Angstrom
30 Blog feed
31 Tests the other team's cornerback

DOWN

1 Send via UPS
2 Currency in the Philippines
3 Asian territory in the board game Risk
4 Actual
5 "30 Rock" network
6 Way of getting things done
7 Production at the Met
8 Sultry Sophia
9 Eats very well
13 Text that might elicit a "no prob" response
16 Finally emerge
17 Following
18 Kills, in mythology
19 "Yowzers!"
20 Hawaiian's gift
22 Parts of a cat's paws
23 Sacred bird of the Nile
24 Nudge
25 They baa
27 Student's number: Abbr.

ACROSS

1 Sent a reminder email to, say
7 Resort wing
10 Beer that's also a movie shout
11 Easy card game to play
12 Person who's always saying "We should hang out!" but never actually follows up
14 "What a ride!"
15 Keep away from
16 "The Joy Luck Club" author
17 On fire
21 ___ off on (pass an obligation to)
22 Guy's mates
26 What 12-Across puts on
28 "This ___ travesty!"
29 "The Hunt for Red October" novelist
30 New wave band whose letters sound out a word meaning "bliss"
31 England's University of ___

DOWN

1 Viral video warning
2 State with six sides
3 Hockey trick
4 TV show set in Ohio
5 Will Ferrell film
6 Pointer Sisters hit with the line "Baby, make your move"
7 Hard work, in metaphor
8 Symbol of China
9 Eve of "Grease"
13 Wall-climbing plant
16 Fierce warriors
17 Attach
18 Talk a big game
19 Flower that's also a color
20 Mean person
22 Garments for Caitlyn Jenner
23 Silver and Goldman
24 "There was this time when ..."
25 Underworld river
27 Winter condition

ACROSS

1 Northern neighbor of Cambodia
5 Remote control button
10 Uninteresting
11 Region of southeast England
12 Alternative to LaGuardia
14 Man with a Mohawk
15 For each
16 Deals with the situation
19 Dunham who wrote "Not That Kind of Girl"
20 French yeses
21 Fey and Turner
22 And so forth, for short
23 Get a look at
24 Where D.C. United plays
29 Two-door car
30 Subdue, in a way
31 Person who chooses to live abroad
32 Only country that starts with O

DOWN

1 Successor to the first three letters of 12-Across
2 TV alien of the 1980s and '90s
3 Mighty tree
4 Wags a finger at
5 ___ Plus (brand of shampoo)
6 Scary snake
7 Tennis tournament won in 2015 by Flavia Pennetta
8 Sister of Venus
9 Crowd scene members
13 Org. with agents
16 Put pressure on
17 Be more clever than
18 Pay, as the tab
19 Wasn't truthful with
21 Iced stuff
23 Proofreading mark
25 Hydromassage facility
26 What "sum" means in Latin
27 Women's World Cup champs of 2015
28 Fellows

ACROSS

1 TV chef Bobby
5 Some storage spaces
10 Bizarre art
11 Group of eight
12 First season
14 Sends to the canvas
15 When the plane will probably land, for short
16 Guys
19 Stain
20 Playlist holder
21 "The ___ Vista Social Club"
22 "Double Fantasy" singer
23 Not him
24 Adele's "19" is one
29 Be
30 Part of town
31 Hard to climb
32 Is worth it

DOWN

1 Dime dome
2 Language spoken in Southeast Asia
3 Hassle
4 Talked and talked
5 Performs
6 Unflinching
7 "Remington ___" (1980s show)
8 Diane or Michael
9 Levels
13 Apple platform
16 Two-terminal devices
17 On deck
18 The ___ Brothers ("What a Fool Believes" band)
19 Sack material
21 Arthur of the stage and screen
23 Address letters
25 Find work for
26 Clothing with a hook
27 180° turn
28 More for Cubans

ACROSS

1 Studio with a roaring lion
4 "You talkin' to me?" actor
10 Time
11 Feature of some relationships
12 Where some fruit grows
14 Remove coding errors from
15 Wilma's man
16 Enjoys a frozen pond
18 Tire stuff
23 Zoo enclosure
27 Tropical flavor
28 Where the buyer must beware
30 Maine city
31 ___ out a living

32 Quick
33 First word of a state capital

DOWN

1 Joins together
2 Language whose alphabet has 24 letters
3 Terrifying snake
4 Hazard
5 Chick's home
6 Soft ball
7 Composer Stravinsky
8 Five-star review
9 Piece in the paper
13 Unable to beat the throw to first
17 Too sweet
19 Prickly part of a flower
20 Made hay
21 Bring to mind

22 Set of charges
23 Two-time World Series champs
24 Opposite of "no rush"
25 DNA piece
26 Slight advantage
29 Fish and chips fish

ACROSS

1 "For Your Eyes Only" singer Easton
7 Tiny bit
10 Tries to persuade
11 Mono-
12 George Clooney movie that's also a poker hand
14 U. of Tennessee team
15 Check for weapons
16 Crows
17 Sprint Cup org.
21 Lunchbox cookies
22 Get rid of
26 Las Vegas casino that's also a poker hand (that beats 12-Across)
28 Morning hrs.
29 Planet orbited by Oberon
30 Univ. classroom helpers
31 First-born

DOWN

1 1970s–80s show with Martin Short and John Candy
2 Twinkie's cousin
3 "My Name Is ___"
4 Former loves
5 Called when delivered?
6 Request
7 Capital on the Mediterranean Sea
8 Inner turmoil
9 Othello pieces
13 Brother of Ethan Allen or George Gershwin
16 One of Spain's four official languages
17 Skim
18 Coffeehouse lure
19 Creator of the Sneetches
20 ___ anglais (English horn)
22 With a small and boring crowd, as a nightclub
23 Russo or Descartes
24 Burden
25 "I'm over here!"
27 Address letters

ACROSS

1 Jazz offshoot
4 Ohio city
10 Penny prez
11 Wish you could be more like
12 Like some countries
14 Clicked communication
15 Intentions
16 "The Satanic Verses" author Rushdie
18 Enter your username and password
23 What tobacco chewers do
27 Hawaiian Punch fruit
28 The largest 12-Across country
30 "Eureka!"
31 Newswoman Curry
32 Family cars
33 Install, as carpeting

DOWN

1 Hay bunches
2 Biden's boss
3 ___ colony
4 SMU's home
5 Fuss
6 Place to work out
7 ___ torch (luau item)
8 Utah city
9 Beatty and Flanders
13 Lower, as lights
17 Some people work them
19 Gloomy guy
20 Birth-related
21 The former Mrs. Trump
22 Au pair
23 Alternative to a snowboard
24 Google cofounder Larry
25 ___ Lacoste (former clothing brand)
26 "See ya!"
29 Relations

ACROSS

1 Shorten, often
5 Selected
10 Automaker with a four-ring logo
11 Too-long sentence
12 Good thing to do in life
14 Kid's shout
15 Kyle's brother, on "South Park"
16 Some shelters
19 Low blow
20 Musk of Tesla Motors
21 Shows nervousness
22 Dragon roll ingredient
23 Basketball's trajectory
24 What you won't do if you 12-Across
29 Author Asimov
30 Aleve alleviates it
31 Maryland athletes, for short
32 Try to make a profit on

DOWN

1 "Dig in!"
2 "Everyone knows that!"
3 Name in Ugandan history
4 Squeaky character
5 Study the night before
6 "Whadja say?"
7 "Long Day's Journey Into Night" playwright
8 Absorb
9 "___ Game" (Orson Scott Card novel)
13 Daily ___ (political blog)
16 Judge to be necessary
17 "Pretty ___?"
18 Shirt part
19 For example
21 SAT cousin
23 The basics
25 Once around the rink
26 Ingredient in many Starbucks orders
27 Org. for checkers
28 Singer Lana ___ Rey

ACROSS

1 Battle
5 ___ metabolic rate
10 Strict memorization
11 Function
12 Laudatory poetry
13 Hit the ball straight at the shortstop, say, with "out"
14 Oscar nominee for "Rambling Rose," "Wild at Heart," and "Alice Doesn't Live Here Anymore"
16 Not in the studio
17 Where there's no disputin' Putin
22 10-time NBA All-Star
25 Amass, as quite a bar tab
26 Kicked off the payroll
27 A.L. West player
28 Suckling pig's food source
29 Expensive
30 Exxon, once

DOWN

1 Role for Elijah
2 "Le Penseur" sculptor
3 Bothered internally
4 Words sometimes separated by a slash
5 Battle site of July 21, 1861
6 It covers 8.7% of the Earth's surface
7 Sahara stuff
8 Got better, as whisky
9 Was winning
15 Abba's genre
18 Participate in a roller derby
19 Big rolls
20 Proposals
21 Be beneficial for
22 Fair
23 Before, to Brutus
24 Positive
25 They might write up freshmen

ACROSS

1 Airport terminal area
5 Sharp
10 Take home
11 Cleaner component
12 Gerald Ford impersonator of "SNL"
14 Mombasa is there
15 Benevolent order
16 Unexpected
17 Quiet room
19 Once around
20 They're on the right
23 Single
26 Cooler brand
28 Compact since 2009
30 #1 ballad for the Rolling Stones
31 Separate thing
32 Have a long sit
33 Complicated and unpleasant situation

DOWN

1 Insurance lizard
2 Oohed and didn't stop there
3 The way things are going
4 Wish you could trade places with
5 Opening trio
6 Lyrical Leonard
7 Range through Eurasia
8 Job at hand
9 Former lovers
13 Seinfeldian "et cetera"
18 For the ages
19 Possessive on blue jeans
20 Backside muscle
21 Radiates, as charisma
22 Whitman's sampler?
23 Damage

24 "That's awful!"
25 Danish toy company
27 Unsmiling
29 By this point

ACROSS

1 Right away, on "ER"
5 Has the gumption
10 Not "for here"
11 Person booted from the country
12 Country on the Strait of Hormuz
13 Sired, in the Bible
14 Cabinet feature
16 Martin Luther's 95 ___
17 Archipelago pieces
22 Russian submarine maneuver featured in "The Hunt for Red October"
25 "What're ya gonna do about it, pal?"
26 Cola Wars side
27 Excellent
28 Ingvar Kamprad's company
29 Software plug-in
30 Watch, as the goal or the bar

DOWN

1 Wilt the ___ (basketball nickname)
2 Holy book
3 Staring, poetically
4 Acting awards
5 "Clair de Lune" composer
6 Gives a pink slip to
7 Latvia's capital
8 Dash
9 Fully prepared
15 Take and use, as an idea
18 Permitted
19 Draw out
20 "Is this seat ___?"
21 "Slammin' Sammy" before Sosa
22 Bean ___ (tofu)
23 Longtime senator Harry
24 Bullets
25 Business that offers treatments

ACROSS

1 Web feed
4 Spoken
10 Currency before the euro
11 "The Night of the ___" (Tennessee Williams play)
12 Crook with a getaway car nearby
14 Prepare to store, as a sailboat
15 Uses a needle
16 Dryer effect
18 Sources of wool
23 Blue hue
27 Tricky picture
28 What the wheelman does in the getaway car, after the heist
30 Soon-to-be adult
31 Opposite of WSW
32 Most dependable crews
33 Once around the track

DOWN

1 Picture puzzle
2 Sparse
3 Jazz composer named for an Egyptian god
4 "Aeneid" poet
5 Driving force
6 Massages
7 1995 pig movie
8 From the top
9 Metallica drummer Ulrich
13 First aid ___
17 Sky puffs
19 Police alert, for short
20 "What's Happening!!" mom
21 Stadium
22 Throat problem
23 "Waterloo" quartet
24 Walk out on the job
25 Strong desire
26 Paul who sang "Diana"
29 Hoop

1	2	3	■	4	5	6	7	8	9
10			■	11					
12			13						
14				■	15				
16				17	■	■	■	■	■
■	■	■	18		19	20	21	22	
23	24	25	26	■	27				
28			29						
30					■	31			
32					■	33			

ACROSS

1 Jungle jumpers
5 Smallest
10 Central or Gorky
11 Make some changes to
12 Intentionally breaks the rules
14 Future man
15 Judge in mid-1990s news
16 He was Mr. Spock
19 Netflix rival
20 Jewelry rock
21 Astronomy wonder
22 Flat screens, e.g.
23 Shoelace feature, when tied
24 Go fourth, in baseball
29 Goodbye, in Geneva
30 First name in the Montgomery bus boycott
31 Furnishings
32 6/6/1944

DOWN

1 Phone fun
2 Buddy
3 Period of the past
4 VIP's place in a stadium
5 Kenny Rogers #1 hit written by Lionel Richie
6 Rival/brother of Peyton
7 Hotel feature
8 Make a home
9 Test drive
13 ___ latte (coffee shop order)
16 "I'm impressed!"
17 Seek to conquer
18 Otherworldly type
19 Hughes or Stern
21 2012 Olympics organizer Sebastian
23 Hazy memory
25 Decision maker
26 Move your head up and down
27 'Merica
28 Fork over the cash

ACROSS

1 Relaxed
5 Cat with an "M" pattern on its head
10 Oil bloc
11 Banish from the country
12 Classic car reintroduced in 2011
14 Intent
15 A thousand thou
16 Washing container
19 Funny Carvey
20 Heavy metal
21 Aspect
22 Chunk of turf
23 McKellen of "Gods and Monsters"
24 What you might make in a 12-Across
29 Not called for
30 Neither none nor all
31 Changes some words in
32 In one's apartment, say

DOWN

1 Kernel holder
2 Friend of Homer
3 Maui flowers
4 2008 opponent for Obama
5 Period in office
6 "Crime and Punishment" weapon
7 Alternative to a Whopper
8 Magician David
9 Give a serious earful to
13 Relatives
16 Seafood soup
17 Approximately
18 "Same here!"
19 Language that's also a breakfast food
21 Not close
23 Alibi ___ (excuse makers)
25 Reduce funding to
26 Sludge
27 "Intriguing ..."
28 Starting point in golf

ACROSS

1 Go wrong
7 Professor's letters
10 Continent for Italia and Deutschland
11 Vowels promising payment
12 Potentially a teacher's least or most favorite student
14 Whistler's offering
15 Computer clicker
16 Dude ranch ropes
17 Made of maple, maybe
21 Neckerchief alternative
22 Word after dramatic or culinary
26 Another term for 12-Across, which I just made up now but you have to admit it sounds amusing
28 "___ Baby" (Toni Morrison novel)
29 As an example
30 Poet's "before"
31 Paid, as the bill

DOWN

1 Religious group
2 Real humdinger, back in the day
3 Gulf state
4 Mug for the camera
5 Company called "Brown" in its ads
6 Yellow eater of dots and ghosts
7 Highly holy
8 "In what way?"
9 Beach barriers
13 ___ Angeles Kings (NHL team)
16 Expel, as steam
17 Be a poor steward of resources
18 Golden award
19 Earth tone
20 "Scooby-___, Where Are You!"
22 ___-Caribbean
23 Tree part
24 Vocal quality
25 Vehicle made for snow
27 Bathroom, to Brits

ACROSS

1 Dimes' fractions of dollars
7 Had more points than
10 Sick and tired of everything
11 Longoria of "Desperate Housewives"
12 Hack
14 Aboard
15 Fail to be
16 Viagra rival
17 Unpaid worker
21 India's first prime minister
22 Japan's sixth-largest city
26 Like 12-Across?
28 Tribe for whom a U.S. state is named
29 737 maker
30 Not later
31 Coworker of Doc and Bashful

DOWN

1 Emerald City curtain-puller
2 "___ Almighty" (Steve Carell movie)
3 Barbershop shout
4 Emerson, Lake & Palmer, e.g.
5 Concealed
6 Use all your might
7 Video game part
8 "___ knew that!"
9 Pub game
13 Common tax shelter
16 Bottom-of-the-toaster stuff
17 As a joke
18 Super-cool
19 Tossed
20 Prior to, in verse
22 Patella's place
23 Dog on the comics page
24 Car pioneer Karl
25 Hip
27 Charged particle

ACROSS

1 ___ scheme (shady financier's trick)
6 Fellow
10 Constellation for which a movie studio was named
11 Extreme anger
12 Bartles & Jaymes product
14 Attorney General's domain: Abbr.
15 Chip shot's path
16 Gusto
18 Towns
22 Put back to zero
24 In need of a hot bath
25 Deep pan
27 "Now it's all clear," in three letters
28 What you might need if you hold a 12-Across too long?

32 Home to Hanoi, Hyderabad, and Hiroshima
33 Willing to believe anything
34 Like bad cake frosting
35 Use 140 characters or fewer

DOWN

1 Baby ___
2 Baltimore bird
3 They're hard to see on Halloween night
4 "Avatar" actress Saldana
5 Ancient Peruvian
6 Iris family plant
7 Linden or Holbrook
8 Birthday candles reflect it
9 Apiece

13 Sphere
17 Dawn brings one
19 Rent sharer, casually
20 Mourn
21 Whispered words
23 Drag along
26 "Critique of Pure Reason" philosopher
28 "Hee" or "Yee" follower
29 Naked ___ jaybird
30 Reject
31 Uncooked

ACROSS

1 Tennis shot to buy repositioning time
4 ___ number
10 Freezer cubes
11 Meeting items
12 Outstanding student's achievement
14 Danger
15 Soccer ___ (parents with minivans)
16 Can't look away
18 Amount of medicine to take
23 Former New York Mets home field
27 Poisonous substance
28 What students who get 12-Across aren't doing in class
30 Cartoon redhead
31 Big bird
32 Command
33 Fish eggs

DOWN

1 Voice features
2 Two quartets, when combined
3 Beloved Yogi
4 Harnessed the wind
5 One of a dozen
6 Diane of NPR
7 "___ Thin Air" (Jon Krakauer book)
8 Genesis man
9 Highlands girl
13 You're using it right now (I hope)
17 Part of USSR
19 One of 100 in D.C.
20 Ire
21 Mechanical device, casually
22 Follow
23 Healing wound
24 Aesop's napper
25 Mark indelibly
26 Muscle hassle
29 Casual greetings

ACROSS

1 Space between two things
4 "Friends" friend
10 Like some skater kids
11 "Messiah" composer
12 Chophouse entrée
14 Poe's middle name
15 Burden
16 Greatest hits
18 Detective from Japan
23 "Sighted sub, sank ___"
27 Supporter of the arts?
28 Piece of sports equipment for kids
30 Conan the barb-arian?
31 Pond fish
32 Have $200 coming to you, in Monopoly
33 "You ___ My Sunshine"

DOWN

1 Do pretty well on the test
2 Walk casually
3 Betting arrangements
4 Wunderkind
5 Antepenultimate word of "Casey at the Bat"
6 Atop
7 Garden in Genesis
8 Male lover
9 Part of BPOE
13 D.C. ballplayer
17 California city from the Spanish for "ash tree"
19 It may say "Welcome"
20 Japan's third-biggest city
21 One voice
22 Song from way back
23 "Cut it out!"
24 "Thank You for the Music" band
25 Snickers alternative
26 Yale students
29 Part of a journey

ACROSS

1 Where cranberries grow
4 They're tougher with your arms crossed
10 It's all around you
11 Vermont, Virginia, or Ventnor, on a Monopoly board
12 When to go to bed
14 Summary
15 Big test
16 Can't get enough of
18 Person with a divining rod
23 "___ Electric" (Oasis song)
27 Questioning word
28 When drinks are discounted
30 Silverstone of "Clueless"
31 Heavy drinker
32 Pour into a carafe, as wine
33 Next year's coll. freshmen

DOWN

1 Iraq's second-largest city
2 Stopped a squeak in
3 ___-Roman wrestling
4 Drained, as energy
5 It climbs trees and walls
6 Place for un chapeau
7 One operating system
8 Cat that's also a shoe brand
9 Appear
13 Floppy part of an elephant
17 "And?"
19 Another questioning word
20 Dr. who wrote many books
21 False move
22 Takes it easy
23 Fish that spawns in rivers
24 Robust looking
25 Long, dramatic movie
26 Animal shelter
29 Yang's counterpart

ACROSS

1 NATO secretary general Stoltenberg
5 Bee's threat
10 On
11 Easy instrument to play
12 Firecracker named for a fruit
14 Country where most Masai live
15 Poems often written "to" someone
16 Long in the tooth
17 Big boss, briefly
19 Tex-___
20 GoPro feature, for short
23 Cuisine with mee krob
26 One way to wake up
28 Item in an Italian kitchen
30 "But you said ..." retort
31 Thought
32 Phobias
33 Have an inclination (to)

DOWN

1 "The Gloved One"
2 One of the Barrymores
3 Exceedingly
4 Nimble
5 Where eagles soar
6 Forbidden act
7 Clothing brand with an alligator logo
8 Alaska city
9 Oodles
13 Marathon or steeplechase
18 Part of 17-Across, for short
19 Middle-distance runner
20 Indelicate
21 Funny Woody
22 "Sorry about that!"
23 Late-in-the-week exclamation
24 In good shape
25 Song for one
27 To some degree
29 Licenses and passports

ACROSS

1 Paella piece, often
4 Poland's capital
10 Every last drop
11 Animal with a long tail
12 Many a "Boardwalk Empire" character
14 Exhausted
15 Stitched
16 Gave a midterm to
18 Position, as troops
23 Plenty
27 Chengdu's country
28 Fairly easy putt, though not a gimme
30 In an equitable way
31 Wicked cool
32 Chain founded by Dave Thomas
33 Ernie of golf

DOWN

1 "Blue Ribbon" beer
2 Get married in Vegas, perhaps
3 Fleshy plants
4 Became limp
5 Time
6 Wooden floor covers
7 One of the herbs in that Simon and Garfunkel song
8 From the top
9 Alert to danger
13 Palindromic cable channel
17 Fake ducks
19 Food that's hot in Hanoi
20 Petrol amount
21 Shaq of NBA fame
22 You need 10 for a first down
23 Several

24 Not recorded beforehand
25 Kiln
26 Be inclined (to)
29 Enjoy a jet

ACROSS

1 "Hey, you!"
5 One of two on the human face
10 "Portnoy's Complaint" novelist Philip
11 Econo ___ (motel chain)
12 Stench
13 Constellation of a hunter
14 Tricks to draw the infielders in
16 Attached a patch, maybe
17 Birds on a pond
21 Tricks on fourth down
25 Simple
26 Panetta, Russell, or Spinks
27 Edge
28 Fallon succeeded him on "The Tonight Show"
29 Rocky peaks
30 Whole bunch

DOWN

1 College teacher, for short
2 Fizzy drinks
3 Add fuel to, as a fire
4 Did a quarterback's job
5 Become foggy
6 Car's warning
7 Work on an article
8 They may clash
9 Barbie's buddy
15 Adorns with ornamentation
18 Thins out the pack
19 Prepare to propose, perhaps
20 Rock
21 Jamie of "M*A*S*H"
22 Thailand is there
23 Chess piece that's never captured
24 Winter whiteness
25 The English channel?

1	2	3	4		5	6	7	8	9
10					11				
12					13				
14			15						
	16								
			17		18	19	20		
	21	22	23						24
25					26				
27					28				
29					30				

ACROSS

1 Clothing with hooks
5 Rot
10 Where to get a pastrami on rye, light mustard
11 Coffee shop feature
12 Sort of
13 ___ town (like a recent arrival)
14 Potato variety
16 Shorthand takers
17 Equilibrium
22 Parent's permission-denying phrase
25 "That's false!"
26 Christmas
27 Word before space or limits
28 Not fooled by
29 Nonpoetic writing
30 Votes in favor of

DOWN

1 Annual celebrations, for short
2 Make a counter-argument against
3 Similar
4 Squash
5 ___ rap (Spotify genre)
6 "Milk's favorite cookie," according to ads
7 Home for Golden Grahams or Peanut Butter Cap'n Crunch
8 In the center of
9 Marino or Rather
15 What you have early in a football game
18 Bug
19 Oliver who directed "JFK"
20 "Can ___ Witness"
21 Songs without vocal harmony
22 Not my
23 Walkman-wearer on "The Simpsons"
24 Finds work for
25 M-Q connectors

ACROSS

1 Rice dish
6 Butter amounts
10 Occupied
11 Working hard
12 Spooky
13 Information
14 With fervor
16 Mambas and cobras
17 Cover completely
21 With envy
25 Just plain bad
26 Aircraft brand
28 Michael of "Arrested Development"
29 Instrument with a keyboard
30 Helen's city
31 Gets closer to

DOWN

1 Dessert cooling on a window sill
2 Don Juan's mother
3 Set bait for
4 Largest of the seven continents
5 "___ Good" (Chuck Mangione song)
6 Italian city where "The Taming of the Shrew" is set
7 Had ___ to do (was focused at work)
8 Book jacket feature
9 Sticks around
15 Beating, but just barely
17 Kick out
18 Not even once
19 Second-largest city in Africa
20 Soothe, as concerns
22 "Milord"
23 One of its letters stands for "Golf"
24 MMXVI, for one
27 They give meds

ACROSS

1 Pig sounds
7 D.C. United, Montreal Impact, et al.
10 Santa's syllables
11 Yes, to Celine Dion
12 John Denver classic
14 Shear fabric?
15 Celebrity whose last name is unnecessary
16 Entryways
17 Planet with beautiful rings
21 Fad
22 Joel or Ethan
26 Famous fans of a golf legend
28 Egg ___
29 Tempt, as customers
30 Roll of the die, sometimes
31 Like some bread

DOWN

1 George Bernard ___ (Irish playwright)
2 Forbidden act
3 "Whoops!"
4 Agitate
5 Not just "a"
6 "We must be leaving" response
7 Demi or Roger
8 Moon-related
9 Exasperated sounds
13 Secret agent
16 With openness
17 Insufficient
18 Feature of many road signs
19 Dance for two
20 Machine gun name
22 Irene who sang the theme to "Flashdance"
23 Rocks worth mining
24 Give off
25 Cultural rival of L.A., CA
27 Take to court

ACROSS

1 ___-Man (1980s video game)
4 Kid's toy
10 ___ Dhabi
11 Lizard some keep as a pet
12 Maine dinner garment
14 "The First Time ___ Saw Your Face"
15 Allows
16 It symbolizes debt
18 San Francisco's baseball team
23 Rights org.
27 One-named entertainer
28 Skewered food
30 NBA great Abdul-Jabbar
31 Eggs, to a biologist
32 Scattered, as a population
33 Nighttime furniture

DOWN

1 More bloodless
2 Higher than
3 Cut into pieces, sometimes
4 Naming as a reference
5 Get better, like wine or cheese
6 Knitting loop
7 Kaplan of "Welcome Back, Kotter"
8 Pound or ounce
9 Catches, as a crook
13 ___ Lanka (Asian island nation)
17 Words on a sign you put on someone's back
19 "Now I get it!"
20 Tycoon
21 Treasure ___
22 Really awful
23 Inquires
24 Fellow
25 Italian money, before the euro
26 Computer owner
29 "For ___ a Jolly Good Fellow"

ACROSS

1 Beatles album with an exclamation point
5 "What goes around, comes around" concept
10 Plant in some shaving creams
11 Liberates
12 28-Across, in other words
14 ___ pole
15 Organized
16 Place where pigs live
17 Simple bed
19 Health bar grain
20 Harvard rival
23 Restaurant head
26 Work with students
28 12-Across, in other words
30 Funny Fudd
31 5,280 feet
32 Anchors
33 Event with discounted items

DOWN

1 Knife handles
2 Poet on whose work "Cats" is based
3 Like some goals or ideals
4 Tennis great Sampras
5 Colonel Sanders' place
6 "___ we all?"
7 Actress Russo
8 Prefix with physics
9 Abbr. in many job titles
13 Certain community center
18 Palindromic man's name
19 Deal
20 One of the Obama girls
21 Poker announcement
22 Number of little pigs
23 Science class, for short
24 Part of an angel costume
25 Tickle Me ___ (1990s doll)
27 Shady trees
29 Medical professionals, for short

1	2	3	4		5	6	7	8	9
10					11				
12			13						
14					15				
16				17	18				
			19				20	21	22
23	24	25			26	27			
28			29						
30					31				
32					33				

ACROSS

1 Top celebrities
6 Creature you should check yourself for after hiking
10 Cowboy's event
11 Eight, in Spanish
12 Number of hours in the day or ribs in the human body
14 Baltic, Mediterranean, and Arabian
15 Part of a pound
16 Future falcon's home
18 Musical genre from Jamaica
19 "___ Doubtfire"
22 Chemist's workplace
24 The five main vowels
26 Right now, in four letters
30 A lot to spare
32 Not on time
33 More competent
34 Pair that may be blue
35 Movable mall business

DOWN

1 ___ and crafts
2 Rob of "Wayne's World" and "The West Wing"
3 Concept
4 Hearing, touch, or taste
5 Young person
6 Cubes in Japanese cuisine
7 Desktop images
8 Norris or Berry
9 Pyongyang and Seoul's peninsula
13 Class where you do the downward dog
17 Oversupply
19 Tree for syrup makers
20 Race with a baton
21 Seven, in Spanish
23 Title deer
25 Bills given as change
27 By yourself, or a brand of plastic cup
28 God of war
29 Fringe benefit at work
31 Animal that also means "talk endlessly"

1	2	3	4	5		6	7	8	9
10						11			
12				13					
14				15					
		16	17			18			
19	20	21		22		23			
24		25			26	27	28	29	
30				31					
32				33					
34				35					

ACROSS

1 Rival of ABC
4 Was the first band to play
10 Just fine
11 Tropical fruit
12 They may be drunk at dessert
14 Connect with
15 Redeem, as a check
16 Frames
18 Got misty-eyed, with "up"
23 Billing abbr.
27 "I was at work all day," for example
28 What you can't make 12-Across with?
30 Alluring quality
31 Tolkien beast
32 Elapse, as time
33 Some Windows systems

DOWN

1 Groups of actors in plays or movies
2 David who sang "Starman"
3 Clay pigeon used in shooting
4 Decide not to be a part (of)
5 Hound's hand
6 For the ages
7 Granny
8 Emoticon colon
9 Quick running race
13 Spielberg creatures
17 ___ whites (beautiful teeth)
19 Pie ___ mode
20 Wisconsin college, or to speak harshly about, in slang
21 Movie critic Roger
22 Frisbees
23 Very quickly, for short
24 Nightclub in a Barry Manilow hit
25 Recipe amounts
26 Three, in Spanish
29 Shoot the breeze

1	2	3		4	5	6	7	8	9
10				11					
12			13						
14						15			
16					17				
				18		19	20	21	22
23	24	25	26		27				
28				29					
30							31		
32							33		

ACROSS

1 Person from Salt Lake City or Provo
7 Manets and Monets, say
10 Alabama city, or a kind of phone
11 Armed conflict
12 Poster child, as for a cause
14 Immediately, in the E.R.
15 North ___ (troubled nation)
16 Littlest
17 Petrified
21 Put a levy on
22 Tie, in chess
26 Film noir character, often
28 In the past
29 Gave for a while
30 Cruise of "Mission: Impossible"
31 Put emphasis on

DOWN

1 They call strikes and balls
2 Aggressive street seller
3 Swedish band that sang "Waterloo"
4 Sword part
5 Boxing great
6 Smooched in the back seat
7 Not in the dark
8 Marathon, steeplechase, and 100-yard dash
9 Halloween option
13 In favor of
16 Olympic awards
17 March 17 man, for short
18 What some planes carry
19 Tried and true saying
20 Amp (up)
22 First word of many letters
23 Glassmaker Lalique
24 Yes votes
25 Takes down the aisle
27 Wee child

ACROSS

1 Place for a cat
4 John Updike or Anne Tyler
10 Letters before a crook's alias
11 Desire that one will
12 3'9" actor
14 Constellation with a three-star belt
15 Conks out, like an engine
16 Didn't have an oversupply
18 Impatient sound
23 Different
27 Hugh Laurie show
28 Role for Gene Wilder or Johnny Depp
30 Popular shrub
31 You're breathing it
32 Quarterback called "Broadway Joe"
33 Michael Che's show, for short

DOWN

1 Childbirth
2 "Ran" man Kurosawa
3 Sarah from Alaska
4 "Let's give it a shot!"
5 Plunder
6 Apple tablet
7 Garr of "Young Frankenstein"
8 Suffix with luncheon or kitchen
9 Rogers and Campanella
13 "Hahahahaha"
17 Muted trumpet's sound
19 Cutesy-___
20 Sushi fish
21 Open the door for
22 Necklace sphere
23 McGregor of "August: Osage County"
24 Minnelli of "Cabaret"
25 Poetry event
26 Singer Fitzgerald or Henderson
29 Thus far

ACROSS

1 Swordfight wound
5 Red ___ (pizza brand)
10 Amazon Prime rival
11 Love, to the French
12 Kind of golf club
13 Last entry in kids' books about the alphabet, often
14 iPhone sound
16 Kickoff prop
17 ___ and reel
18 Animal whose butter is eaten by Mongolians
19 Part of a skirt
22 Totally tubular pasta
24 Similar
26 Peak point
27 Like game show rounds, often
28 Viral phenomenon
29 Complicated
30 Breyers competitor

DOWN

1 Polo, say
2 Marie with two Nobel Prizes
3 "Are you ___?"
4 Step on a ladder
5 Shoulder weapon
6 Make changes to
7 Judge Judy wears one
8 "___ House" (Crosby, Stills, Nash & Young classic)
9 Gun safety class org.
15 "Hamlet" or "Macbeth"
18 "Zowie!"
19 Had dreams
20 Sworn foe
21 Combines
22 Wheel features
23 Unexciting
24 24-hour mini-bank
25 Make up a story

ACROSS

1 Not many
4 "Goodness!"
10 Firewood chopper
11 "I'm over here!"
12 1988 baseball movie
14 Oscar winner Redmayne
15 Silent entertainer
16 Close back up, as a Ziploc bag
18 Healthy
23 X-rated material
27 Prefix with grade or liter
28 "Not That Kind of Girl" memoirist
30 Good grade
31 Mike and ___ (theater candy)
32 Watch a Weimaraner, say
33 Apiece

DOWN

1 Fictional "Animal House" college
2 Give off, as energy
3 Binds together
4 "Sweetie"
5 The solver of this crossword
6 Slow wiggler
7 "Didn't see ya there!"
8 Wander near and far
9 Stadium feature
13 "The dog ate my homework," e.g.
17 Creature in a swarm
19 Affleck of flicks
20 Square
21 Dracula's fear
22 Microwave oven feature
23 Hit with an open hand

24 Crazy Frog or Melodramatic Chipmunk
25 Foot, inch, or pound
26 Landscape colors
29 Expensive violation of the law

ACROSS

1 "Finding ___"
5 Funnywoman Sykes
10 "Victory is mine!"
11 Letter-shaped piece of metal
12 12:00, half the time
13 Nuts
14 Creator of Hogwarts
16 Real jerk
17 Grapeseed or canola
18 Starbucks drink
19 Sports equipment made by Rossignol
22 Oscar winner for "Whiplash"
25 High points
26 Bar orders
27 Oregon's capital
28 In ___ of (replacing)
29 Catty, as comments
30 Being unproductive

DOWN

1 Man in black
2 Fuzzy creatures from the forest moon of Endor
3 Invaders of Spain
4 ___ occasion (never)
5 Kate Middleton's man
6 Intensely stirred up
7 Element #10
8 "Shoot!"
9 Sedaris or Schumer
15 Pity party phrase
18 Made a reproachful sound
19 Reliable
20 Prepare to propose
21 Edition of a magazine
22 ___-Claude Van Damme
23 Hindu goddess
24 Timbuktu's country
25 NYC learning centers

ACROSS

1 Influenced
7 "Law & Order:___"
10 Classic sports car
11 Counterpart to 20-Down
12 Famous line from "Poltergeist"
14 Painters' vehicles
15 Kind of power
16 Solemn sounds
17 Start making all your shots
21 Last box to check on a form, maybe
22 "Cut it out!"
26 "It'll be all right!"
28 Greek "T"
29 Not knowing right from wrong
30 Pen stuff
31 Place for some body piercings (ouch!)

DOWN

1 Comedy show from 1976 to 1984
2 "So funny!"
3 "Absolutely!"
4 Is worth it
5 Go astray
6 "It ___ matter"
7 Snail's home
8 How some YouTube videos go
9 Manipulative people
13 Tool with a flat blade
16 Like bibimbap and kimchi
17 "Teflon Don" John
18 Hawke of "Boyhood"
19 London's land
20 Counterpart to 11-Across
22 ___ till you drop
23 U. of Maryland athlete
24 Spoken
25 World Cup hero of 1958 and 1970
27 "Don't tell me anything else about this!"

ACROSS

1 "Bill & ___ Excellent Adventure"
5 Israeli city
10 It fittingly rhymes with "cram"
11 "Go this way" sign feature
12 Washington, Jefferson, Theodore Roosevelt, and Lincoln are on it
14 Pasta sauce brand
15 Finishes up
16 Small amount
17 Cousin of Inc.
19 Louvre Pyramid architect
20 Central, when used with another word
23 Mountain cat
26 Shire resident
28 Serious, like 12-Across?
30 Like pretzels
31 Kind of carpet
32 "Still Crazy After All ___ Years"
33 Healthy looking

DOWN

1 Be alluring
2 Additional charge
3 Had the nerve
4 Self-satisfied
5 "That's a laugh!"
6 ___ and dangerous
7 Hotel room item
8 Name on many old pickup trucks
9 Leaves amazed
13 Only
18 Lovers' quarrel
19 Slacks
20 Word on a Starbucks menu
21 Perfect
22 Keep away from
23 "Hey, buddy!"
24 Four Corners state
25 Long-term spy
27 Skin breakout
29 Look over

ACROSS

1 Home country of world chess champion Magnus Carlsen
7 Birthday card figure
10 Go too far with
11 Catch, as a suspect
12 Sound heard in a tub
14 "Do I have to draw you ___?"
15 "The ___ sauce"
16 Got closer to
17 Start of a JFK quote
21 Mrs. ___ (North Pole resident)
22 Consisting of two parts
26 Chewing gum brand
28 Bird that can't fly
29 Jacket parts
30 One way to get web access
31 "___ an idea!"

DOWN

1 Romance novelist Roberts
2 Latin word for "egg"
3 Singer McEntire
4 Alternative to a sandwich
5 Make a sum
6 "Sure thing!"
7 Words separated by a slash
8 First aid kit stuff
9 Receded, as a tide
13 Thick snake
16 Like some diets
17 Had pains
18 Poor areas of a city
19 Afghanistan's capital
20 Heart of the matter
22 Trick
23 Company you can get a ride from
24 Having the power
25 Scottish girl
27 Scrooge's word

ACROSS

1 Evening, as the score
6 Nicolas of "Red Rock West"
10 Daltrey or Moore
11 Gem found mostly in Australia
12 Person who saw it all
14 Computerized task performer
15 Part of a lowercase I or J
16 First Best Actor winner ___ Jannings (his name reverses to a fruit)
18 Cop's weapon
22 Hudson and Upton
24 Hand over
25 ___ out an existence
27 Free (of)
28 Person who heard it all (yes, it's a real word!)
32 Water, to Juan
33 Summer camp craft
34 Stage award
35 Animal known for its laugh

DOWN

1 Alex with all the answers
2 Cellist who teamed up with Bobby McFerrin
3 "Understood!"
4 Never before seen
5 Part of a crossword
6 Cold medicine brand
7 Chimpanzee or gorilla
8 Food for a Ford
9 Ernie who won the British Open in 2012
13 Tater ___
17 Room for error
19 Calm
20 Inventing Thomas
21 Moses parted it
23 Schuss around moguls
26 ___ A Sketch
28 Nosh on
29 In the past
30 Point, in baseball
31 Vote against

ACROSS
1 "Get outta here!"
6 Cheese that's made backward? (literally!)
10 John who sang "Dear Abby"
11 Dark drink
12 South Carolina resort town
14 Record label founded in 1931
15 Court
16 Musical with the song "La Vie Bohème"
18 Coffee break time
22 Rarin' to go
24 Living room piece
25 Grammys category
27 Uninteresting
28 Kind of shark you might spot in the waters of 12-Across

32 One of the woodwinds
33 Michelle, Malia, or Sasha
34 Garden growth
35 Comedian Dave or former Speaker of the House Tom

DOWN
1 ___ of influence
2 Yalta's peninsula
3 Agitating
4 Tiny crawler
5 "Let's play the laser pointer game again!" or "How about changing my litter box already?"
6 Rebounding sounds
7 Jane or John
8 In the manner of

9 Magazine with "Spy vs. Spy"
13 "___ really"
17 Named
19 "I won't accept those terms!"
20 House shaped like a letter
21 "Help!"
23 Actress Charlotte
26 Univ. teacher
28 In what way?
29 Prez on the penny
30 Tavern owner on "The Simpsons"
31 "Girls" network

1	2	3	4	5		6	7	8	9
10						11			
12				13					
14				15					
16		17		18		19	20	21	
22			23		24				
		25		26		27			
28	29	30			31				
32				33					
34				35					

ACROSS

1 Long tooth
5 Notes in the office
10 Completed
11 Cairo's country
12 Mountaintop structure
14 Reggae relative
15 Sean Lennon's middle name
16 Informs
19 Major journey
20 Long or Lewis
21 Mazatlán mother
22 Tax-deferred setup
23 First Supreme Court chief justice John ___
24 Thrower of barrels
29 Backbone
30 Dayton's state
31 Watches, as the goal
32 Certain performance-enhancing drug, for short

DOWN

1 On behalf of
2 "Selma" director DuVernay
3 Actor Beatty
4 Horrific
5 Self-referential
6 Self-importance
7 "Heavens!"
8 First game in a series
9 Golf shot
13 Gives approval to
16 Desert desire
17 Home to Rome
18 Preamble
19 12th president
21 ___ 'n' cheese
23 Namath and Montana
25 Come to a conclusion
26 "Now it all makes sense!"
27 Nintendo system
28 Indicate "yes"

ACROSS

1 Expensive California city
7 That man
10 World's second-longest river
11 "Without further ___ ..."
12 Cheese on pizza
14 It's between Caps Lock and S
15 Hilarious DeGeneres
16 They're pretending
17 "Black Beauty" novelist
21 Chum
22 Pottery class stuff
26 Cheese on crackers, salads, and even pizza
28 Wolfed down
29 Acting president?
30 Mustachioed "Simpsons" character Flanders
31 "Boston ___"

DOWN

1 Doll's cry
2 Run ___ (go wild)
3 Sit around
4 "Miami Vice" role
5 Nonvenomous snake
6 Hard to believe
7 Berry with an Oscar
8 Unambitious type
9 Complains
13 Animal with antlers
16 Stuns
17 Carl who wrote "Cosmos"
18 Overact
19 Tech magazine
20 Hard-boiled item
22 Former dictator
23 Insignia
24 "The Imitation Game" subject Turing
25 Yin's counterpart
27 Pickleball barrier

ACROSS

1 Sounded like an angry cat
7 "Exodus" Oscar nominee ___ Mineo
10 James Cameron hit
11 Paid athlete
12 What you thought the shingles on top of your house were ...
14 Wasn't in the dark
15 Bank robbery
16 Supermarket sections
17 Shock
21 Like some cheddar
22 Cheese that rhymes with "cheddar" (with a Boston accent)
26 ... and what you did when it rained and you found out they weren't

28 Suffix with govern or steward
29 Get payback for
30 Having slightly less money than necessary for a purchase
31 Playground equipment for two

DOWN

1 Bird with exceptional eyesight
2 Russian form of John
3 Make happy
4 Dinner in a bowl
5 One of two on the head
6 TV shrink
7 Ruin
8 Came up in conversation

9 Brooklyn apartments, sometimes
13 Hi-___ graphics
16 Top males or females
17 Tray stuff
18 Band with a flavor of Ben & Jerry's named for them
19 Fall guy
20 Gallery works
22 Untethered
23 Long periods of time
24 Senator's garment
25 Not many
27 Night before

ACROSS

1 Epic tales of adventure
6 Wheat or quinoa
10 Journey with a goal
11 "I'm open! Pass it!"
12 In prison, in slang
14 Small batteries
15 Floor cleaner
16 Dove of poetry or Moreno of movies
18 Was guilty
22 Wear down, as resistance
24 Have a snack
25 Poem often about a person
27 Play about Capote's life
28 Easy way to kayak
32 Not pro-
33 Tabloid person
34 State of disarray
35 "Beverly ___ Ninja"

DOWN

1 Credit card processing service
2 Nanny
3 Bothers
4 Hardwood tree
5 Part of a flower
6 Help fund the cause
7 Gun, as a motor
8 Valuable mineral
9 Apiece
13 Fisherman's need
17 Handsome fellow
19 "I can't wait to hear this!"
20 Country on the Mediterranean Sea
21 "I'm all ___!" (clumsy person's lament)
23 Mag workers
26 Mark for good
28 It's built by beavers
29 Undivided
30 Pounds and kilograms: Abbr.
31 Outdoor sports store

1	2	3	4	5		6	7	8	9
10						11			
12				13					
14				15					
16		17		18		19	20	21	
22			23		24				
		25		26		27			
28	29	30			31				
32				33					
34				35					

ACROSS

1 Caveman diet
6 Chihuahua sounds
10 Defendant's claim
11 Slimy vegetable
12 It rolled through Old West towns
14 Mischief maker
15 Carl Yastrzemski of the Red Sox, for short
16 Change bills
18 Consumer advocate Nader
22 Half of a record
24 Yodel lookalike
25 Title sitcom creature
27 Wedding promise
28 Scary swarm
32 "Intriguing ..."
33 Leave alone
34 The Who or the Guess Who
35 "See you around"

DOWN

1 Backyard features
2 Donors to a university, usually
3 Walked with difficulty
4 Go back
5 Like a salad, maybe
6 "My goodness!"
7 Cold War prez
8 Ante-
9 Pathetic
13 Van Gogh was missing one
17 Where a sunken ship lies
19 Lyle of country music
20 Moon of Saturn
21 Role for Neil Patrick Harris
23 100%
26 Lost your footing
28 Palindromic piece of clothing
29 Letters sometimes seen in red, white, and blue
30 Word on a bathroom door
31 Arthur of "The Golden Girls"

ACROSS

1 Clothing in Kolkata
5 "Awesome!"
10 Overflow (with)
11 Japanese city
12 Part of an archipelago
13 Turned toward
14 Result of someone getting cut off in traffic, maybe
16 Stratego piece
17 Homer's pop
18 Lines of praise
19 Atlas page
22 Juicer's nasty behavior
24 Shopping center
26 Currency of Belgium and Greece
27 Poe poem, with "The"
28 All tied up
29 Be
30 ATM charges

DOWN

1 Mixes together, as ingredients
2 Slave who told fables
3 Send along, as information
4 Typed notes to
5 Where a guest may sleep
6 Operation
7 Speed
8 Supplement, with "out"
9 Totally cool, dude
15 Glowing
18 Gives off, as charm
19 Pale purple
20 See it the same way
21 The peasantry
22 ___ Shankar (Norah Jones's dad)
23 Diving location
24 Not post-
25 Not strict

ACROSS

1 Modeled for the camera
6 Scottish family
10 Not the same
11 Sacred
12 Person who's always at the office
14 "___ is me!"
15 Republicans, for short
16 Former GM brand
18 Toyota hybrid
22 Mae and Adam
24 Actress Kendrick
25 Strong tree
27 Unpleasant strain
28 Person who's always at the candy store
32 Bird of prey
33 Stopped sleeping
34 Places to stay
35 Fresher

DOWN

1 Meeting
2 Peter of "Lawrence of Arabia"
3 Does away with, as incriminating documents
4 "I just saw a mouse!"
5 Pain in the neck
6 Deep Deepak
7 Chat room chuckle
8 Big boxer
9 Largest metropolis in the U.S.
13 Use one leg
17 Puts on the shelves, as merchandise
19 Source, as river water for a lake
20 Facebook button
21 Teacup holder
23 ___ Paulo, Brazil

26 "Start Trek II: The Wrath of ___"
28 Life force, or a Greek letter
29 Largest ethnic group in China
30 Possess
31 Be in arrears

ACROSS

1 Speedy
5 Playful animal
10 Voice that means "high"
11 Overhead
12 Country whose leader is parodied in "The Interview"
14 Run after
15 Poindexter
16 "That's awesome!"
17 Ang or Peggy
19 High school transcript number
20 ___ and reel
23 Gravity-defying haircut
26 One thing you can do with a crossword clue (like I just did there)
28 African country formed in 2011
30 Online magazine edited by Julia Turner
31 Longtime soft drink brand
32 Race with teams
33 Tiny weight

DOWN

1 Top of the line
2 The ___ State (Hawaii)
3 Adoptable cat
4 Highchair users
5 Tree in many city names
6 Steak with a letter
7 Ripped
8 At any point
9 Take in some Tolkien
13 Lend a hand
18 Pair next to your hair
19 Must, casually
20 Company with yellow trucks
21 Nebraska's largest city
22 Jean jacket material
23 Cold War country
24 Person from Warsaw
25 Having two uses
27 Put on the clothesline
29 "Whaddya think you're doing?"

ACROSS

1 Sheep peep
4 Bites hard
10 Common street name
11 "Messiah" composer
12 4.00, for many valedictorians
13 "That's the truth!"
14 Graceful animal
16 Scary strain
17 "Such a pity!"
21 Person from Copenhagen
22 Turn to the side, as one's gaze
23 Name for a newspaper
25 Take back
28 Big wheels
29 "Jane Eyre" novelist
30 Wrath
31 ___ tank
32 Opposite of "oui"

DOWN

1 Asked for alms
2 South American animal
3 World's largest rainforest
4 Cook-off food
5 One of the rooms in the board game Clue
6 Not working for a while
7 Docs
8 Princess's "problem"
9 Sneaky
15 Graceful
18 Admits
19 Maestro Toscanini
20 Spielberg or Pinker
22 Ancient Mexican
24 Not pro-
25 They score TDs
26 Before, in poetry
27 Person with a badge number

ACROSS

1 Split ___ soup
4 Like some medicine or tea
10 24-hour bank feature
11 Baltimore baseball bird
12 One of the great apes
14 Consume, as resources
15 Marina structure
16 Daniel or Tom
18 ___ Mifflin (company on "The Office")
23 Businesses that sell treatments
27 Wynonna Judd's mom
28 One place you're unlikely to find a 12-Across
30 Each
31 Airport guess, for short
32 Empty ___ (kind of goal in soccer or hockey)
33 Get a look at

DOWN

1 Steps
2 Actor/screenwriter Hawke
3 Friendship
4 Moved like a bunny rabbit
5 Time period
6 Watermelon cover
7 Clown name
8 Baldwin or Waugh
9 Vegetable used in potato soup
13 Water + dirt
17 Marathoner, e.g.
19 Henpeck
20 Catches some Z's
21 Act theatrically
22 ___ Janeiro
23 Bridge's length
24 ___ Le Pew (cartoon skunk)
25 Working hard
26 Editor's mark
29 Winter hazard

ACROSS

1 Take off to get hitched
6 Unruly crowds
10 Copy machine company
11 High hairdo
12 It spins over your head
14 "Letters from ___ Jima" (2006 Clint Eastwood movie)
15 Roof material, sometimes
16 Starbucks size
18 Sister of Desi Arnaz Jr.
22 Look over lasciviously
24 Cat with no tail
25 Food for a Ferrari
27 ___ Beta Kappa (honor society)
28 They lie under your feet
32 Lightning ___
33 Dodge, as a disaster
34 Autobahn auto
35 Information amounts

DOWN

1 Thrill
2 Room to be creative
3 American League East bird
4 Senator or congressman, e.g.
5 Illuminated sign, in a theater
6 Big gun
7 Light switch setting
8 Sports ___
9 Kid, sometimes
13 Zero, in soccer
17 Bela of "Dracula"
19 Pill form
20 "Where are you?" response
21 Is
23 4, on some holes
26 Guesstimate
28 Cherbourg's country: Abbr.
29 Holtz or Costello
30 Strange
31 Wall climber

1	2	3	4	5		6	7	8	9
10						11			
12				13					
14				15					
16			17		18		19	20	21
22			23		24				
		25		26		27			
28	29	30			31				
32				33					
34				35					

ACROSS

1 Ways off the highway
6 Impersonates
10 Emerge
11 Patron saint of sailors
12 Game show where the host says "Survey says ..."
14 Its HQ is the J. Edgar Hoover Building
15 Cost
16 Navel stuff
18 Gets on video
22 Ready to roll
24 Based in reality
25 Agent, for short
27 Pitcher's number
28 Reality game show where contestants perform stunts
32 Therefore
33 Triangle or trapezoid
34 Highway hazard
35 Giggle-evoking class

DOWN

1 Drawing
2 Desert land
3 Performing without words
4 Greek letter
5 ___-contained
6 Opposite of victory
7 "Excellent work!"
8 Big bird
9 Piece of the lawn
13 "However ..."
17 Horrified emotion
19 Before Uncle Sam takes his cut
20 Croatia's continent
21 Prepared, as a tuna steak
23 Ump
26 Emulate Tom Brady
28 D.C. agent
29 Prior to, to poets
30 Get better, maybe
31 "The Motorcycle Diaries" role

ACROSS

1 Cuisine that uses a lot of peanuts
5 Swedish cars
10 Swedish tennis star
11 Dog on "The Jetsons"
12 Nickname for especially loud and enthusiastic fans at a football game, after 22-Across
14 Poem of praise
15 Shark's giveaway
16 Croc's cousin
19 Hand over
20 Soul great Redding
21 Two-time Oscar winner Dianne
22 See 12-Across
23 Spy novelist Fleming
24 When 12-Across might get especially loud
29 Architect known by his initials
30 Pennsylvania city
31 School worries
32 Monthly bill

DOWN

1 When people post retro pictures on Facebook, for short
2 "In what way?"
3 "___ you kidding?"
4 Homes made of ice
5 Make happy
6 ___ Wednesday
7 Charge for some twenties
8 Hair features
9 Poetic form used by Shakespeare
13 Prez on the dime
16 Took up an exercise program
17 Not out on the town
18 Traffic jams
19 Ash
21 Baby's cry
23 "Indeed!"
25 No longer working: Abbr.
26 Stuff in a mine
27 Take the biggest trophy
28 Piece of hockey equipment

ACROSS

1 ___-Robbins
7 Civil War side, briefly
10 Unlike couch potatoes
11 Rawls or Albano
12 It has 64 squares
14 Skirt parts
15 Come together
16 "Gosford Park" director Robert
17 It separates Africa from the Arabian Peninsula
21 Estrada and Spoelstra
22 Ancient stringed instrument
26 It has 64 writing implements, often
28 "You've Got Mail" company
29 Accumulate, as work left undone
30 Letters on the 7, on some phones
31 Pizza-by-the-slice chain

DOWN

1 "Brandenburg Concertos" composer
2 Dull pain
3 Part of a flower
4 Smooch
5 RNs insert them
6 Latin for "cloud"
7 State to be true
8 In a way
9 Poet W.H.
13 Toronto's province: Abbr.
16 "___ Fables"
17 Summarize
18 Blunder
19 Uses an old phone
20 Plane's place
22 Chorus syllables
23 Rideshare company
24 Guided event
25 Trade event
27 Ad ___

ACROSS

1 Red-breasted birds
7 Curved path
10 Present giver's demand
11 Black or Baltic
12 Person traveling in Europe, often
14 Benevolent lodge
15 "___ done it again!"
16 Burst like a balloon
17 Harriet of the Underground Railroad
21 World Cup winner of 2006
22 Birds in the Harry Potter books
26 Thief who may target a 12-Across
28 ___-mo camera
29 Philip Morris, now
30 Money in Japan
31 Jump to attack

DOWN

1 Spa garment
2 October stone
3 Grammy winner for "Morning Phase"
4 Printer fluids
5 Small amount, as of brandy
6 Remain with the company
7 Invite to one's apartment
8 Superman portrayer
9 Wasn't unconcerned
13 Officer
16 Company cofounded by Peter Thiel
17 On the way to being drunk
18 Of value
19 Beloved strips
20 Jan. honoree
22 Prefix meaning "eight"
23 Cincinnati radio station, in a 1970s sitcom
24 Luke's sister
25 Right away, in the ER
27 "Wonderfully done!"

ACROSS

1 Door holder
5 O. Henry's ___ Kid
10 Enormous landmass
11 Poe's middle name
12 It may be served with mint jelly
14 Female in a flock
15 Pod item
16 Levels
19 Sounds from a displeased crowd
20 Ford explorer?
21 Thick
22 Greek consonant
23 Letters that promise repayment
24 At personal risk
29 "Turn that ___ upside down"
30 Part
31 Talk show set plants
32 Had in one's hands

DOWN

1 Pickle holder
2 Naked ___ jaybird
3 Open ___ Night
4 Business that's rolling in dough
5 Light lunch location
6 Under the weather
7 Apply quickly, as a layer of paint
8 Uncredited appearances
9 At first, maybe
13 Pained shouts
16 Start of a basketball game
17 Guard against damage
18 Copy cat?
19 William Blake's poetic paradise
21 Film noir classic
23 Places to crash for the night
25 Possess
26 Extreme anger
27 Country singer Tillis
28 Horrific

ACROSS

1 Quickly
6 Country singer Church
10 Group of witches
11 John's "Two Virgins" collaborator
12 Lewis Carroll twin
14 Totally dominate in competition
15 The sun
16 Easy victory
18 Slander, but in print
22 Work hard
24 Moore or Lovato
25 Coffee holder
27 Jennings of "Jeopardy!" fame
28 Sylvester's nemesis
32 "My Name Is ___"
33 Statistics calculation
34 Body scan
35 Utah city

DOWN

1 Stage stars
2 Meeting
3 Grand road
4 Letter between "bee" and "dee"
5 Completes
6 Peeper cover
7 Fishing need
8 "I like ___" ('50s campaign phrase)
9 Cedar Rapids college
13 "how did u get so funny"
17 Without much spirit
19 Treat others well
20 Come to the forefront
21 Deciduous tree
23 Egyptian king of long ago
26 Lamb in your hands

28 S.E. Hinton book
29 Boring card game
30 Time for a historian
31 Cancel, as plans

ACROSS

1 Sacha Baron Cohen character
6 Wine container
10 Nonsensical
11 Ashtabula's state
12 Celebrities
14 www.army.___
15 Night before
16 From the top
18 Ann ___, Michigan
22 Tree that's a symbol of Lebanon
24 Like bad losers
25 Deli sandwich
27 "Apocalypse Now" setting
28 People with many followers on a certain social networking service, in a pun on 12-Across
32 ___ Forest

33 One of the Chipmunks
34 They may have it
35 Car in a Beach Boys song

DOWN

1 Whopper rival
2 Surfing the web
3 Spoke harshly (against)
4 Unwelcome kitchen visitor
5 Head: French
6 Apple ___ (kitchen gadgets)
7 "Now I get it!"
8 Grab a chair
9 Garden pond fish
13 Sister of Zsa Zsa
17 Doesn't use efficiently
19 Comet rival

20 Eloquent speaker
21 Cause to think (of)
23 Wagon wheel mark
26 Top-of-the-line
28 Airline until 2001
29 Path
30 Mike and ___ (candy brand)
31 Tease

ACROSS

1 Taters
6 "Dancing Queen" Swedes
10 Hosts in an apartment
11 Ones for the road?
12 Hawaii's nickname
14 Get with a laser
15 Ronan Farrow's mom
16 Power cards
18 "Get outta here!"
22 Restaurant stack
24 Gambling game
25 MBA holder, maybe
27 Attention, in metaphor
28 "Forever Young" band
32 Sarcastic laugh
33 "Later, skaters"
34 Puts two and two together?
35 Last sound of "flamingo"

DOWN

1 Magician's shout
2 Queen's quarters
3 Tournament won four times by Martina Navratilova
4 "I knew that!"
5 Emails hopefully "caught"
6 Go after
7 Feather ___
8 Lunch with a crunch, for short
9 Bar pour
13 "Pretty sneaky, ___!"
17 For instance
19 Land, as a fish
20 Kind of watch
21 To an even greater degree
23 Arabian, Baltic, or Caspian
26 ___ Office (part of the White House)
28 "Now I see what you mean!"
29 Young fellow
30 The third degree?
31 Words with a ring to them?

ACROSS

1 ___ Talks (popular online lectures)
4 "___ Weapon 4"
10 Time of the past
11 Goddess born wearing full armor
12 Their center boxes are free
14 Two quartets
15 Kid stuff
16 Have breathing trouble
18 Champaign's twin city
23 Blood ___
27 Make changes to
28 First-born Beatle
30 Kind of skating
31 56, once
32 Take care of, as a bar tab
33 Was winning

DOWN

1 Kneeling Tim
2 Psychologist ___ Fromm
3 "Inferno" author
4 "Tao Te Ching" author
5 And so on: Abbr.
6 Not this
7 Knight in shining armor
8 Warhol with wacky wigs
9 Girl in a glen
13 "Amazing!"
17 Chalkboard item
19 Sandwich usually on white bread
20 To any extent
21 Guts
22 Deodorant brand
23 Blood's gang rival

24 Chinese women's tennis star who won the French Open in 2011 and the Australian Open in 2014
25 "If ___!"
26 "Weekend's here and I am ready!"
29 Yoko born in Tokyo

ACROSS

1 "Would you like a receipt?" askers
5 Best Picture of 1958
9 "Whoops!"
10 Computer button
11 Kelly of daytime talk
12 How a hotel's size is measured
13 Good starting hand in Texas hold'em
15 It's over your head
16 Ask too many questions
17 Yonder woman
18 Airport named for a prez
21 Lovely but frosty lady
23 December song
25 Part of a window
26 Dullsville
27 Just a single time
28 All there
29 Demand

DOWN

1 Surrounding glows
2 Dense
3 In a funk
4 Former Lakers great, for short
5 Like good chocolate chip cookies
6 Champion's shout
7 Nice rock
8 They await your return
10 Class you need before taking another class, for short
14 Did not reverse, as a judicial ruling
17 Breakfast biscuit
18 Diplomat Kirkpatrick
19 Seller of stolen goods
20 Got in the groin, maybe
21 Country on the Persian Gulf
22 "Once ___ a time ..."
23 "The Big Bang Theory" network
24 In the style of

ACROSS

1 Seven-time National League MVP
6 Couch potato's place
10 Regarding
11 McGregor of "Amelia"
12 Director of "The Miracle Worker" and "Bonnie and Clyde"
14 Baby's garment
15 "However ..."
16 Relaxed sigh
18 Wood used to make nonalcoholic beer
22 Mountain range with a brand of candy named for it
24 Virgin or RC
25 Spending limit
27 Permit
28 One who may work behind bars
32 Money for freedom
33 Wake up
34 ___ of Good Hope
35 Raised, as the stakes

DOWN

1 Sheep's sound
2 Patrick who wrote "Master and Commander"
3 Better than people expected
4 "Thank you, Captain Obvious"
5 Proof you bought a ticket
6 Infected
7 Be behind
8 Adorer
9 Advising Landers
13 Massage
17 Mock, as a stand-up comic
19 Prepare to put away, as a sleeping bag
20 John of "A Fish Called Wanda"
21 Loathing
23 Stopped standing
26 Neighbor of Brazil
28 Network since 1922
29 Battery size
30 Quick hit off a flask
31 Cut (off)

ACROSS

1 "___ it obvious?"
6 Actor Julia of "The Addams Family"
10 Dominant
11 Trade fair
12 Yes, tentatively
14 Camel color
15 ___ Vegas Review-Journal (Nevada's largest newspaper)
16 Concludes
18 Sushi fish
22 Vacuum cleaner brand
24 He defeated Clay to become U.S. president
25 Graphic designer's computer choice, often
27 Sailor's home
28 No, tentatively
32 Coordinate
33 Witherspoon who coproduced "Gone Girl"
34 Jersey material
35 Goes the distance

DOWN

1 Passed the time
2 New York city
3 Shells out
4 Vancouver Canucks, Edmonton Oilers, et al.
5 Rearmost part
6 Increases the level of
7 Swung tool
8 FedEx rival
9 Bathroom, in Britain
13 Gobble up
17 Such a huge amount
19 Snacks (on)
20 Division that includes the O's and the BoSox
21 Enjoys a frozen pond
23 Capture
26 Computer key in the lower left
28 Ending for real or surreal
29 Easter egg stuff
30 Iron-___ (patches)
31 Shaken Sweet ___ Lemonade (Starbucks drink)

ACROSS

1 Expand, as a highway
6 Lane or Lowry
10 NSX automaker
11 R8 automaker
12 "Six Degrees of ___" (1993 movie)
14 "Boardwalk Empire" channel
15 Simple bed
16 ___ Blanc (highest of the Alps)
18 Stands against a wall
22 Additional
24 Get off ___-free
25 Game with Skip cards
27 Highest heart
28 Six Degrees of ___ (movie game)
32 "Indeed!"
33 Be
34 Sir's counterpart
35 William Butler ___

DOWN

1 Words written into a dirty car window
2 Freezer
3 Chemical company
4 Period of time
5 DEA source
6 Drinks made with milk
7 Yes, to Yvette
8 Wedding day phrase
9 Greed or gluttony
13 "You've Got Mail" company
17 Wise saying
19 Shrub originally from Australia
20 Free item's quality
21 Heart implants
23 Combative Coulter
26 Follow orders
28 One of the Kardashians
29 Greek vowel
30 By way of
31 Body spray brand

ACROSS

1 Cracker
6 Get more and more angry
10 Musical set in Buenos Aires
11 Very, dahling
12 "Gone Girl" actor
14 Atlanta current-events giant
15 Not yet determined, for short
16 A loooong time
18 Like people from Galway or Killarney
22 Gangster Lansky
24 Karenina or Kournikova
25 Little battery
27 Yankee great Gehrig
28 California's governor
32 Guinness or Waugh
33 Wish you could have
34 Well-heeled
35 Acts

DOWN

1 Laptop feature
2 Retaliate for
3 Albert in "Annie" and "Skyfall"
4 Guess at the airport, for short
5 Simple watercraft
6 Toyota model
7 Not merely "a"
8 Computer key in the upper left
9 Panda Express pan
13 Org. featured in many thrillers
17 ___ engine (Bing or Yahoo!)
19 Head over heels
20 Pulled a fast one on
21 Favored hangouts
23 Sunbeam
26 Multiple choice test choices
28 Peanut butter container
29 Inventor Whitney
30 Camcorder button letters
31 Fish eggs, at a sushi bar

1	2	3	4	5		6	7	8	9
10						11			
12					13				
14				15					
16			17		18		19	20	21
22				23		24			
			25		26		27		
28	29	30				31			
32					33				
34					35				

ACROSS
1 Lacking energy
7 "___ the Dog"
10 Brunch drink
11 www.smu.___
12 Art class brand
14 Aegean and Adriatic
15 Starbucks sizes
16 Secret meetings
17 Santa's cry
21 Send your taxes in online
22 Waterfront sight
26 Wet blanket
28 Mao ___-tung
29 Go back (on a promise)
30 "What can I do for you?"
31 Literary collection

DOWN
1 Iowa city
2 World's longest river
3 Jane Austen classic
4 Tavern that Homer Simpson frequents
5 Neighbor of Egypt: Abbr.
6 Cuban strongman
7 Water sources
8 Grown-up
9 Shot in the dark
13 Like someone who is "out"
16 "___ All Gonna Laugh at You!" (Adam Sandler album)
17 One of the Smurfs, or a trash bag brand
18 Handy to have around
19 Finds a secret spot

20 Ancient
22 Groan-inducing jokes
23 Concept
24 Hip
25 "Marble" loaves of bread
27 ___ Moines (Iowa's capital)

ACROSS

1 Took it easy
7 iPhone download
10 When glaciers advanced
11 2011 kids' movie, or the city it was set in
12 "Last Train to Clarksville" band
14 Section
15 Gill or Vaughn
16 Like some arguments
17 Its last letter stands for "racing"
21 Award for Eddie Redmayne
22 Gymnastics great Korbut
26 Subway Series team
28 Fellows
29 "Silkwood" actress
30 Superlative suffix
31 San Jose's NHL team

DOWN

1 Cracker with seven holes
2 Reverberating sound
3 Spotted
4 Unexciting
5 Driving force
6 "The Mile-High City"
7 "___ you the one who always said ..."
8 Newspaper article
9 Mugged for the camera
13 Korean car company
16 Give a hard time to
17 "Find somebody else!"
18 Fireplace remnants
19 Hint
20 Caribbean islet
22 Slimy vegetable
23 Creepy look
24 Chess lover, maybe
25 Venomous vipers
27 To the ___ degree

ACROSS

1 Painting Picasso
6 "This is terrible!"
10 Belted constellation
11 River with Blue and White sections
12 Show about Superman
14 Pizzeria owner in "Do the Right Thing"
15 West African food
16 Apartment
18 Phoebe of "Gremlins"
22 Singers sing into them
24 Song with the line "I'm not the world's most masculine man"
25 Letters before an alias
27 D.C. ballplayer
28 Where so many exciting things happen
32 It's between theta and kappa
33 Picky ___
34 Prizes, in slang
35 Has fun in the snow, maybe

DOWN

1 Creature that plays dead
2 Nice suit
3 "Blossom" and "The Big Bang Theory" actress
4 "Ha ha!"
5 Just
6 Bat, cat, or rat
7 Word in many rappers' names
8 100%
9 Get a look at
13 Rug cleaner, for short
17 It's steeped in a cup
19 This evening, on a marquee
20 On cloud nine
21 Half-men, half-goats
23 Enjoy fresh powder
26 Seemingly forever
28 Frank McCourt's follow-up to "Angela's Ashes"
29 "___ come?"
30 Its middle letter stands for "time"
31 Shortstop Ripken

1	2	3	4	5		6	7	8	9
10						11			
12					13				
14				15					
16			17		18		19	20	21
22				23		24			
			25		26		27		
28	29	30				31			
32					33				
34					35				

ACROSS

1 Hits (on the head)
5 Hogwarts professor
10 Org. for which many lawyers volunteer
11 Its capital is Cardiff
12 Game designer/ novelist Stephenson
13 Forestall, as a disaster
14 "School of Rock" actor
16 With 17-Across, early tie score in a set of tennis
17 See 16-Across
18 "Be My Yoko ___" (Barenaked Ladies song)
19 Costume department piece

22 Lead singer on "Seven Nation Army"
25 "Divine Comedy" poet
26 Besides
27 ___ demons
28 "Famous" cookie maker Wally ___
29 Sees for the first time
30 Michigan or Winnebago

DOWN

1 Appalachian instrument
2 Separator of continents
3 Peyton or Park
4 Feel sorry for yourself
5 Tiny bird

6 Fleet-related
7 "Here's the Thing" podcaster Baldwin
8 Fringe benefit
9 1970s fad with "sessions"
15 Persons of interest?
18 Combined pair of quartets
19 Fred's redhead
20 "No worries"
21 Flock in a V formation
22 One of the Fondas
23 "You Needed Me" singer Murray
24 Get better
25 Lower, like lights

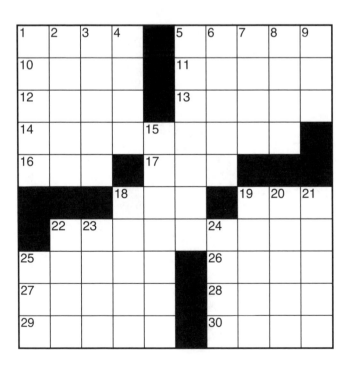

ACROSS

1 West/Clooney/ Keaton/Bale/Kilmer role
7 Boxer's hand
10 Finland, Portugal, etc.
11 Middle words of similes
12 They often contain campgrounds
14 Second-year student, casually
15 Command to the band
16 Words on a Valentine's Day candy heart
17 Specialty of some attorneys
21 When your rights may be taken away?
22 Get beat

26 Where thrashers rule
28 Like wallflowers
29 Test the quarterback's arm
30 Obnoxious person
31 Decrease

DOWN

1 Mrs. Harry Truman
2 Car
3 Leave no escape
4 Light-seeking creature
5 Great ___ House (National Zoo building)
6 Your sister's boy
7 First episode of a miniseries
8 Say "Would you like to see my house?" to
9 Be inefficient

13 Competition for Aqua-Fresh
16 Just plain rotten person
17 ___ coin (let fate decide)
18 Egyptian crosses
19 They show bones
20 Permit
22 Cheryl or Alan
23 Cookie with its name on it
24 Throw off, as survey results
25 Stuart Scott worked there
27 Cutesy-___

ACROSS

1 Wrist piece
6 Extinct creature
10 Hawaiian "Hi there!"
11 Currency in Calais and Cologne
12 Sea-to-air traveler, briefly
14 Part of MTWTF
15 That girl
16 ___ cap
18 Highly impressed
22 Mystery writer's award
24 Animal seen leaping on highway signs
25 Deserving
27 City known for its beaches, for short
28 Air-to-sea traveler, briefly
32 Flower that's also part of the eye
33 B+ or B–
34 "Just the facts, ___"
35 I tunes?

DOWN

1 Breakfast food that's also a verb
2 Celebrity lawyer Gloria
3 Playing (with)
4 ___-Town (the Windy City)
5 ___ and Franz ("Saturday Night Live" duo)
6 Stand up for
7 Paris yes
8 OR or ER bosses
9 "That's really cool!"
13 4, on phone keypads
17 Taking pleasure in causing pain
19 Photograph from a plane
20 Creep
21 Gets worn down
23 Take off
26 Fragile dozen
28 Like low-wattage bulbs
29 Ethan Allen's brother
30 By way of
31 Dude

1	2	3	4	5	■	6	7	8	9
10					■	11			
12				13					
14			■	15			■	■	■
16		17	■	18		19	20	21	
22			23	■	24				
■	■	25		26	■	27			
28	29	30			31				
32				■	33				
34				■	35				

ACROSS

1 Did a figure eight, say
7 Take to the stage
10 Shakespeare title role
11 Bar owner often pranked by Bart
12 Way to explore the world online
14 Olympic Stadium player, once
15 Jackson who sang "Control"
16 Take it slow
17 African tree
21 Goodbye, on one side of the Pyrenees Mountains
22 Giamatti of "Sideways"
26 "Road to Morocco" actor
28 Totally fine
29 Artemis or Orion
30 Blog feed letters
31 A.A. Milne's donkey

DOWN

1 Herb served with salmon
2 Fort with tons of gold
3 On
4 Not "for here"
5 Bigger photo than the original: Abbr.
6 Salon service
7 Microwave oven brand
8 Finds a way to handle the situation
9 Easily irked
13 Wild West?
16 Tacky
17 Beloved elephant
18 Goodbye, on one side of the Pyrenees Mountains
19 Sty sounds
20 Get on your knees
22 My Little ___
23 Regarding
24 Alternative to Lyft or a taxi
25 Instrument for Orpheus
27 Wish you could take back

ACROSS

1 Preserves container
7 "Madam Secretary" network
10 Black, white, and orange bird
11 Bathroom, in Brighton
12 Fair food
14 Consumes
15 Closet stuff
16 Napa Valley business
17 One of the U.S. Virgin Islands
21 American Airlines ___ (where the Miami Heat play)
22 Part of a process
26 Dehumanizing experience, like an actor's open audition
28 First aid ___
29 Go by
30 Subway stop: Abbr.
31 Did a shampooing task

DOWN

1 It's supposed to be funny
2 Part of town
3 Barack defeated him in 2012
4 Scribbles (down)
5 Every last bit
6 Bring toward the boat
7 Exact copy
8 Tunnel-digging tool
9 One of Michael Corleone's brothers
13 Relations
16 Captain Ahab, notably
17 Flour holders
18 Genetic feature
19 Sporty Volkswagen
20 Most populous province of Canada: Abbr.
22 Look over quickly
23 Nighttime bugle piece
24 Not the same
25 Said "Guilty," say
27 One of the Mannings

ACROSS

1 Marriott and such
7 Sworn enemy
10 Soon
11 Teeny-tiny
12 It mostly eats white-tailed deer
14 Metrosexual, back in the day
15 ___ Paulo, Brazil
16 Wad that's not worth that much
18 Ralph Lauren shirts
22 Word on yellow trucks
24 Outpost
25 "Apocalypse Now" setting, for short
27 She sang one line on the White Album
28 Nature's noisemaker
32 Wise bird
33 Leave alone
34 Exchange vows with
35 Glover and DeVito

DOWN

1 Bat instead of
2 Like some bagels
3 Patted (down)
4 Go back
5 False stories
6 Suitcase attachment
7 Spokeswoman for Progressive
8 Well stuff
9 Will Ferrell movie with the line "You sit on a throne of lies!"
13 Dog's sound
17 Email program button
19 Observe
20 Combative
21 Mall tenants
23 Speedy
26 Prefix meaning "enormous"
28 "That's unreal!"
29 Be in arrears
30 Experienced, maybe
31 "State of the Union With Jake Tapper" channel

ACROSS

1 Stoned
5 Bring home a baby sister, maybe
10 Got a perfect score on
11 ___ colony
12 Marjorie Henderson Buell comic strip
14 Not out of the tournament yet
15 "Intriguing!"
16 Dictionary offering: Abbr.
17 Stomach six-pack
19 Springfield seller of Squishees
20 Recipe amt.
23 Dec. holiday
26 Country
28 Colleague of Captain Kirk
30 John of "Sacrifice"
31 Improvised singing
32 Zero people
33 Try again

DOWN

1 George who cofounded the NFL
2 In an unfriendly way
3 Driver's invitation
4 Home theater component
5 Pint in a pub
6 Sandwich shops
7 Masterwork
8 Beloved Brazilian
9 Factually based
13 Get some air?
18 He killed Hamilton
19 ___-Martin (British sports car)
20 End to the fighting
21 Word with chicken or egg
22 Former planet
23 Marvel Comics group
24 "The Adventures of ___ and Otis"
25 Concerning
27 Its second-largest city was Leningrad
29 Away from WSW

1	2	3	4		5	6	7	8	9
10					11				
12				13					
14						15			
16				17	18				
			19				20	21	22
23	24	25			26	27			
28				29					
30						31			
32						33			

ACROSS

1 Make a pass at
6 Indonesian resort island
10 So amazed
11 CEO, e.g.
12 "A Fish Called Wanda" actor
14 Defiant DiFranco
15 Physicist Thorne
16 Alpha-___ (cereal made of letters)
18 Everything ___
22 Fuss
24 Hatcher of "Desperate Housewives"
25 Half of the NFL
27 "Apocalypse Now" setting, briefly
28 Quesadilla component, often
32 Plant with fronds

33 "It's always something!"
34 Comes out on top
35 Fruits shaped like light bulbs

DOWN

1 Muslim veils
2 Part of the plot
3 Pacific island
4 Have the title to
5 Head holder
6 Honk the horn to warn
7 Body spray brand
8 Clinton defense secretary Aspin
9 Sculpting medium
13 Ad ___ (do improv)
17 Cottonmouths and cobras
19 Swiss city or lake
20 Pencil end

21 Brits
23 Popcorn Nuggets maker
26 Use a cleaver
28 Part of the face
29 Ring king
30 Run a scam on
31 Keep tabs on

ACROSS

1 Tiny amount, as of dust
6 She sometimes sings in Irish
10 Great Gretzky
11 Clever turn of phrase
12 Five-time Best Actress nominee (1931, 1937, 1938, 1940, 1949)
14 Kilmer of "Top Secret!"
15 Hawaiian paste
16 Change a few words
18 ___ poker
22 Showed past the foyer
24 Times gone by
25 Lefty voter, for short
27 Simple place to sleep
28 "Can I respond now?"
32 Netflix rival
33 More pleasant
34 Perched on
35 Song holders

DOWN

1 ___ chair
2 Holiday march
3 Human body's "lens cap"
4 Its first letter stands for "Cable"
5 Retain
6 Home ___ loan
7 Monastery resident
8 Feminine side, in Eastern philosophy
9 Mimic
13 Two, in Tijuana
17 Make a little neater
19 Outré architectural style
20 Worked on pants, say
21 Dinklage and Pan
23 Keanu role
26 Kind of bond, for short
28 "Now I get it!"
29 Wagon wheel's path
30 Band whose last letter stands for "orchestra"
31 Quick swim

ACROSS

1 Bandleader Al
5 Or higher, as in recommended ages for books or board games
10 France Cote d'___
11 Michael of "Hannah and Her Sisters"
12 ___ close second (almost won)
13 Finish
14 2002 Jodie Foster movie
16 1970s space station
17 Mick Jagger's ex
22 Sound from a fast plane
25 37th president
26 TV explorer
27 Motrin competitor
28 Finds work for
29 Defeated in, as a game
30 Not as much

DOWN

1 Instruments at posh brunch places
2 "The Compleat Angler" author Walton
3 Like some eggs or noses
4 Oregon ___ (old computer game)
5 Sharp, as wit
6 iPod model
7 Eminem sampled her "Thank You" for his hit "Stan"
8 Latin word on U.S. coins
9 Energy
15 Place to keep liquor
18 Kareem ___-Jabbar
19 Wild West "rough justice"
20 Apple centers
21 Build up, as a fortune
22 Storage on the plains
23 Beasts of burden
24 Kind of salmon
25 "Yep" opposite

1	2	3	4		5	6	7	8	9
10					11				
12					13				
14				15					
16									
				17		18	19	20	21
	22	23	24						
25					26				
27					28				
29					30				

ACROSS

1 Cassette tape successors, briefly
4 Breakthrough events
10 Cut down, as a tree
11 Biblical prophet
12 Steely Dan album with "Black Cow"
13 Glamorous
14 Pouring phrase
16 She won seven French Opens
17 "American Idol" runner-up Bo ___
21 "Brah"
22 Word in some Starbucks orders
23 "Are you kidding me?"
25 Be so angry
28 Life lines?
29 Elk's horn
30 Terre Haute sch. where Larry Bird played college ball
31 Data senders
32 Volleyball barrier

DOWN

1 Tried to catch
2 "I've been here before" feeling
3 Went from side-to-side
4 Tussle
5 ___ of Man (place between Ireland and Great Britain)
6 Seven-color phenomenon
7 Canine command
8 Spinning devil of cartoons, for short
9 Uncomfortable with new people
15 Hit the mats
18 I am, in Berlin
19 ___ longue
20 Patronize a restaurant
22 "Wayne's World" star
24 "Pardon me ..."
25 Adams or Houston
26 Brian of "Here Come the Warm Jets"
27 Airport abbr.

1	2	3		4	5	6	7	8	9
10				11					
12				13					
14			15						
16						17	18	19	20
21				22					
			23	24					
25	26	27					28		
29							30		
31							32		

ACROSS

1 Singer on "It's the End of the World as We Know It (And I Feel Fine)"
6 Plant used to make rope
10 He works standing up
11 Burn soother
12 Highway hopeful
14 Jeff Lynne's old band
15 Mighty tree
16 Vulcan mind ___
18 Unmissables
22 Vedder of Pearl Jam
24 Bygone National League ballpark
25 Hit the slopes
27 Whatever number of
28 Question 12-Across might ask
32 Beheaded Boleyn
33 "Death Be Not Proud" poet
34 Say it isn't so
35 Some statues

DOWN

1 Get-rich-quick plan
2 Worked hard
3 "Word has it ..."
4 Photo
5 Sound you've already heard
6 Seventeen-syllable works
7 Animal also called a wapiti
8 Bully in "Calvin and Hobbes"
9 According to
13 Denver omelet ingredient
17 Wonderful Walt
19 Green, Carter, and Johnson
20 Lease signer
21 Agree
23 Heart test, briefly
26 Film lover's site, for short
28 Wander (about)
29 Undivided
30 Holiday ___
31 The second person

1	2	3	4	5		6	7	8	9
10						11			
12				13					
14				15					
16			17		18		19	20	21
22			23		24				
		25		26		27			
28	29	30			31				
32				33					
34				35					

ACROSS

1 Big party
5 Winners of a certain TV show
10 "Lonely Boy" singer Paul
11 Brown shade
12 Dangerous activity in the air
14 Island for immigrants
15 Simple shirts
16 "Runaway" singer Shannon
17 "Ooh!" follower
19 Popeyes rival
20 Paul Bunyan's tool
23 Concerning
26 Handed (out)
28 Dangerous crime in the air
30 Word before system or colony
31 Orchestra instrument
32 Tries to find
33 Gentle

DOWN

1 Headquartered
2 Achilles tendon neighbor
3 Ability
4 Pilgrim to Mecca
5 School of thought
6 Swimming pool measurement
7 Mayberry kid
8 Forgetful actor's request
9 Gives in to gravity
13 Letters on fighter planes
18 "Back in Black" band
19 Bald cop
20 Latin for "elsewhere"
21 Element #54
22 Beat by a little bit
23 Scary snakes
24 ___-Ball (Chuck E. Cheese game)
25 Daly of "Gypsy"
27 "Fine, then"
29 Ice Bucket Challenge disease, for short

ACROSS

1 Hosted
6 Quick swigs
10 Word before layer or hole
11 Hawaiian island
12 Game with a doubling cube
14 Three-syllable sandwich
15 ___-mo camera
16 Some August births
18 Lady's love
22 Where you live
24 Airline that serves kosher meals
25 Clumsy type
27 "Born in the ___"
28 "Glengarry Glen Ross" actor
32 Ice in the water
33 "No Man Is an Island" poet
34 Part of DINK
35 Like Roger Federer and Martina Hingis

DOWN

1 Use crutches
2 Pop singer Iggy, or a shrub
3 "Does this hurt?" inquirer
4 Pen stuff
5 Photog's masters
6 "That's enough!"
7 What "sum" means in Latin
8 Soup with sliced beef
9 Baltimore or Toronto newspaper
13 Space bar neighbor
17 Puts fuel in, as a fire
19 Grads
20 Stoneworkers
21 Craft overhead
23 "2001: A Space Odyssey" computer
26 D.C. agents
28 Airport for NYC
29 Punching phenom
30 Fish and chips fish
31 Do the lawn

ACROSS

1 Marsh ___ (people of southern Iraq)
6 Stop from suckling
10 Embalmed communist
11 Round waffle
12 Alert
14 Chinese concept
15 Engage in chit-chat
16 Former magazine or former NBA stadium
18 Attacks
22 Gives chow
24 "___ Man" (Emilio Estevez cult classic)
25 "___ be an honor!"
27 Tear in two
28 "Get up right this instant!"
32 Ogden Nash or William Wordsworth
33 Pound part
34 "___ the night before Christmas ..."
35 Spend lots of time at the mirror

DOWN

1 Many
2 Call something new
3 "Tennis, ___?"
4 Prefix with engineering
5 Cozy
6 It has a sink and running water
7 The self
8 Years lived so far
9 Rejecting words
13 Old-school cheer
17 "The Complete ___ Guide to Crossword Puzzles & Word Games"
19 Unflappable
20 For one
21 Letterman list
23 Name made from three consecutive letters
26 Decide not to discuss any more
28 Decide
29 Not soon or later
30 Vote in favor of
31 Cat's coat

ACROSS
1 Energizer size
4 Leaves no tip for
10 Took a match to
11 Do really well, casually
12 Bob Marley tune
14 It might be airtight
15 Gush
16 Silver medal winner's place
18 Greatest New York Yankee of all time, according to ESPN
23 Can't stop crying
27 Michael of "Dirty Rotten Scoundrels"
28 Dean Martin tune
30 Let go of
31 Comedian Kirkman
32 Old-school Coke container

33 Many a "Law & Order" character, for short

DOWN
1 Different name
2 Supermarket section
3 High level?
4 Alpine activity
5 "___ the season ..."
6 Societal troubles
7 Movie that loses a lot of money
8 Bill of Abraham
9 Simmered food
13 "Last Week Tonight" network
17 The 1850s, say
19 Pork product
20 Spanish red wine
21 Dressed to dazzle, maybe
22 She played Thelma

23 Ticket remainder
24 "This isn't good ..."
25 Thailand's currency
26 OBP or RBI
29 Classic NBC show

ACROSS

1 As an example
7 Sentimental type
10 Much more than several
11 In may be inflated
12 Stuck-at-home feeling
14 Teary twosome
15 Happening
16 They're nice for the nose
17 Ex-husband of Roberts
21 Lend ___ (listen)
22 Jason's ship
26 Why you sometimes can't go outside, and therefore might have 12-Across
28 Shoot the breeze
29 Sent an invoice
30 Resort feature
31 Keeps from being captured by

DOWN

1 Turn toward
2 Beauty product name
3 It comes with a sash
4 Elevator brand
5 Palindromic French word
6 Cause and ___
7 This clue's clue number
8 Representative
9 Baltimore, Los Angeles, and Rotterdam
13 Genesis name
16 Flashy light
17 Homes for lions
18 Like beer in a keg
19 Scooter name
20 Gobble up
22 Rights org.
23 ___ Gold (pretzel brand)
24 Joy
25 2 to 1, for example
27 Canola ___

ACROSS

1 "I'm so busted!"
6 Hairdo
10 Cohesion
11 Sit on the throne
12 "Guitar Town" country singer
14 Played a kids' game
15 ___ sauce
16 Animals raised on Australian farms
18 Dietary restriction, sometimes
22 Home ___
24 Soup ___ (memorable "Seinfeld" character)
25 Part of a journey
27 Awful
28 Decide the party's not for you
32 Be unable to avert your gaze
33 Melodramatic goodbye
34 Afrikaans word for "farmer"
35 Summarize

DOWN

1 Overflowed with pride
2 Punctual
3 Too busy to leave work
4 "Catfish: The TV Show" channel
5 They may be hazel
6 Item in a box of 64
7 Your and my
8 "___ see you later"
9 ATM charge
13 Very long stretch
17 You, right now
19 Cotton or chiffon
20 Yard shrub
21 Clean
23 Stand for the kickoff
26 Equipment
28 Shot with topspin, ideally
29 Narcissist's issue
30 Tavern option
31 Ending for lime or Power

ACROSS

1 Dr. J once played in it
4 Want to be like
10 New dog
11 Make wet
12 Most commonly seen snake in crosswords
13 Nook
14 Party food named for a brand of cereal
16 Catches word
17 Spring sheep
21 Real first name of "Royals" singer Lorde
22 Country on the Mediterranean
23 There's a white rabbit on it
25 ___ strip
28 Choose
29 Part of "OITNB"
30 5 to 5, for example
31 Dog in the ___
32 Stuff used in shipbuilding

DOWN

1 Helicopter named for an Indian tribe
2 Amount of apples
3 Ask for a second trial
4 Second president
5 Creative Catalan
6 The year 2149
7 Event that might make a CEO wealthy
8 Fire up, as a motorcycle
9 Compass pt.
15 What 1969's Best Picture winner "Midnight Cowboy" received
18 Costello's buddy
19 Nearsightedness
20 Cowboy poet Black
22 Big ship
24 Wrath
25 Palindromic woman
26 Time period
27 "The Da Vinci Code" author Brown

ACROSS

1 Steak choice
6 Comes apart
10 "Go this way" symbol
11 Thought
12 Motel chain whose buildings' tops are a specific color
14 "Wow!"
15 Penn of the "Harold & Kumar" movies
16 1990s alt-rock band Better Than ___
18 Irritable
22 Horst of "The Bachelor"
24 Pole, Czech, or Russian
25 Stylistically imitating
27 Brian who produces U2 albums

28 Doll whose top is the same color as 12-Across
32 Las Vegas Strip hotel named for a kind of song
33 Number of eggs
34 Former New York Times crossword editor Will
35 Rain ruins it

DOWN

1 Store sometimes pronounced with a French accent
2 Tropical wind
3 Commands
4 Neither fish ___ fowl
5 Cuddly creature in the "Star Wars" universe
6 Hunter's supply

7 A mean Amin
8 Bic item
9 ___ Diegans (some residents of California)
13 Cracklin' ___ Bran
17 Just for fun
19 Contemptible person
20 Converted into leather
21 De Carlo of "The Munsters"
23 Part of IPA
26 Comes up with sums
28 Like sashimi
29 "Where ___ we?"
30 Card game whose name is spoken upon winning
31 The person reading this crossword clue

1	2	3	4	5		6	7	8	9
10						11			
12				13					
14				15					
16			17		18		19	20	21
22				23		24			
			25		26		27		
28	29	30				31			
32				33					
34				35					

ACROSS

1 Kravitz and Bruce
7 Org. for swingers?
10 Didn't cook at home
11 Operate
12 Neighborhood bar
14 Cairo cross
15 Any Beatles song
16 Bed threads
17 "Let's do it!"
21 Gullible
22 Pad ___
26 Hub
28 Before, poshly
29 Estée of perfume
30 Cleared (of)
31 Not all there

DOWN

1 Random singing syllables
2 Famed prep school
3 Head-body connector
4 2014 biblical epic with Russell Crowe
5 Brynner of "Exodus"
6 Knitwear fashion brand
7 One of the seven deadly sins
8 Put the pedal to the metal
9 Chips before playing
13 "Excellent!"
16 Gets bigger
17 Gather
18 Native New Zealander
19 Chopped up finely
20 Eggs, in Latin class or biology class
22 Sightseeing expedition
23 Go where no one will find you
24 From the top
25 "Well done!" response
27 "___-Man Fever" (hit novelty song of 1982)

ACROSS

1 Buddy
4 Classic 1980s arcade game
10 Early HIV-fighting drug
11 Weather phenomenon with a Spanish name
12 Country whose capital was Belgrade
14 Wash away
15 Manuscript
16 Sound effect
18 Spoke about
23 Pretends
27 "___ do great!"
28 Where you might hear "namaste"
30 "The Breakfast Club" costar of Ally, Molly, Anthony Michael, and Judd
31 Mendes of "2 Fast 2 Furious"
32 Interception catcher, often
33 Fully prepared

DOWN

1 Single-___ insurance
2 Sky blue
3 Second in command in a state: Abbr.
4 Atacama or Kalahari
5 "___ take care of it"
6 Biting buzzer
7 Bar where beer is cheap
8 Bell Labs creation
9 Milk source
13 Song of praise
17 Himbo
19 ESPN analyst Holtz
20 Bros
21 Antipasto piece
22 Enjoy buoyancy
23 Senate votes
24 Common soap opera plot device
25 It's said two days after hump day
26 Word on a store window sign
29 Command to a Chihuahua

ACROSS

1 Cooling units, for short
4 Oscar winner for "The Usual Suspects"
10 Park place?
11 Oil company named for a state
12 Animal that pops its head out of a hole
14 Cut into two equal pieces
15 ___ Lang ("Smallville" role)
16 Ready to roll
18 "The Georgia Peach"
23 Fizzy drink
27 President or prime minister
28 Game where you bonk an animal when it pops its head out of a hole
30 Tuskegee ___ (famed WWII detachment)
31 Card game that's also a drink
32 Packing quite a punch
33 "And still ..."

DOWN

1 Dominant
2 Reef stuff
3 Play for time
4 Bourbon in New Orleans or Beale in Memphis
5 Louvre Pyramid architect
6 Skating move
7 ___ vez ("every time," in Spanish)
8 "The dismal science," for short
9 Mat positions?
13 They keep patients hydrated
17 Evil ruler
19 Magna ___ laude
20 Suffix for a science
21 Contradict
22 Sportscaster Musburger
23 Make an even trade
24 Louisville's river
25 Bull's-eye hitter
26 High point
29 Burns or Watanabe

ACROSS

1 The Guess Who or the Who
5 Home Depot rival
10 Extinguish birthday candles
11 Confident way to solve a crossword
12 Movie from which "The Usual Suspects" took its title
14 "This is so awesome!"
15 Amusing quality
16 Part of a plug
19 Rioja or Orvieto
20 Supermarket hassle
21 Madrid mister
22 Top pitcher in the rotation
23 Clanton at the O.K. Corral
24 Brazilian beach
29 Highly skilled, as soldiers
30 Prominent release of April 3, 2010
31 Some Nordics
32 Yanks

DOWN

1 London channel
2 In the style of
3 Words of rejection
4 ___ Johnson, a.k.a. "The Rock"
5 Flower that's also a girls' name
6 "Snakes ___ Plane"
7 Good for everyone
8 Los Angeles suburb
9 Katarina Witt or Kristi Yamaguchi
13 Cancel, as plans
16 Put
17 Yodeled brand name
18 Bowling ball target, on the first shot
19 Small amount
21 Jamaican music
23 Puts a cold pack on
25 Snarfed down
26 Animated Indian
27 Bring something up for the hundredth time, say
28 Craigslist posts, usually

1	2	3	4		5	6	7	8	9
10					11				
12				13					
			14				15		
16	17	18				19			
20					21				
22				23					
24			25				26	27	28
29					30				
31					32				

ACROSS

1 Calligraphy fluids
5 Complete and total
10 Great Plains protrusion
11 Call up
12 "E pluribus ___"
13 Not on time
14 "Chicago" actress
16 Applied to, as balm
17 Hog, like all the pizza
22 "Chicago" actress
25 Marie who co-discovered radium
26 One of 100 in a Scrabble set
27 Maps out
28 Benedict played him in "The Imitation Game"
29 Tricks
30 Type to, sometimes

DOWN

1 Trooper and Rodeo automaker
2 Good scores, on "The Gong Show"
3 Movie for which Jane Fonda won her first Best Actress Oscar
4 Really, really upset
5 Thus far
6 Compared to
7 Went quickly
8 Winds up
9 King, in Cartagena
15 Unemployed
18 Insinuate
19 Limber
20 "Chill out!"
21 Reznor or Dilfer
22 Last letter, in phonetic alphabets
23 God of love
24 Word in many beer names
25 Chest compressions and breaths, for short

ACROSS

1 Dr. ___ Skoda (J.K. Simmons's role on "Law & Order)
5 Swiss ___ (vegetable)
10 Cover with asphalt
11 Workplace for some clowns
12 Club in a golf bag
13 "___ to tell you ..."
14 Spice used in curries
16 Touchscreen tool
17 Avoid embarrassing yourself
22 Caribbean island just off the coast of South America
24 Amy Winehouse hit
26 Hit the bell
27 Pixelated letter
28 It's about a foot long
29 Writer Dominick or actor Griffin
30 Throw casually

DOWN

1 Long stories
2 French revolutionary killed in the bathtub
3 Tusk material
4 Rival of Connors and McEnroe
5 Harvard color
6 Santa's syllables
7 Levine of Maroon 5
8 Hit the accelerator on
9 Jane or John
15 Loud enough for the ears
18 Before anyone else
19 It borders British Columbia and Utah
20 Some iPods
21 Beats by a little
22 Holier-___-thou
23 Drops on the roof
24 Color of the sun, on Japan's flag
25 Bird farmed for burgers, in Australia

1	2	3	4		5	6	7	8	9
10					11				
12					13				
14				15					
16									
				17		18	19	20	21
		22	23						
24	25					26			
27						28			
29						30			

ACROSS

1 "Dear" lady?
5 Cuban, e.g.
10 Japanese leader during WWII
11 Acrobat maker
12 Bring down to the police station
13 Unwilling to change
14 Alternative to corn starch
16 "Naughty you!"
17 North ___ (less-visited Grand Canyon side)
18 Cost of a service
19 Isn't now
22 Gum flavor
25 Make fun of
26 Affleck flick
27 Funny feeling
28 Creepy look

29 "Someone ___ Story" (song from the musical "Chess")
30 Sit ___ by (fail to act)

DOWN

1 Trip to the plate
2 Uncouth types
3 Singer whose last name is Guðmundsdóttir
4 Singer Ono
5 United, Continental, or American
6 "And you can take that to the bank," e.g.
7 Word with dancer or boots
8 To some small degree
9 ___ Bull

15 Symbols of peace
18 It runs around the house
19 Tech mag
20 Silicon Valley investor
21 Newspaper article
22 "Better Call ___"
23 Shakespeare made hundreds of them
24 Country between Senegal and Niger
25 Not just "a"

107

ACROSS
1 Destiny in life
4 Sorrowful speech
10 Settlers of Catan resource
11 Played slowly, on sheet music
12 Card game cry
13 The son on "Sanford & Son"
14 "Mad Men" actor
16 Name to commit crimes under
17 It's mined in Australia
21 Pig sty
22 Oliver or Sharon of Hollywood
23 Art collector called "The First Lady of Texas"
25 Thief
28 Implore
29 Benjamin's love in "The Graduate"
30 Keg stuff
31 Did a jig
32 Possessed

DOWN
1 River blockage
2 Foraging bird
3 Kei Nishikori's sport
4 Singing syllable pairs, or U.S. soccer star Alexi
5 Smith or Scott
6 Enormous
7 ___ trip
8 Trent Reznor's band, for short
9 Tater ___
15 Like some Jews
18 Muckety-muck
19 She played Jessica on "Murder, She Wrote"
20 Three-___ race
22 Made happy
24 Not yours
25 Home to roses
26 Birmingham's state: Abbr.
27 One of the Bobbsey twins

ACROSS

1 Big hit
5 1-Down author ___ Salten
10 Baseball's all-time leader in grand slams, familiarly
11 Party announcement site
12 Mouthwash flavor
13 Air Force installations
14 Familiar river structure
16 Country on the Med.
17 Blue jeans pioneer Henry David ___
18 Hat named for a city in Africa
19 Passports and such, for short
22 Famous river structure
25 Hooded animal
26 One voice
27 Bonnie who sang "Angel From Montgomery"
28 Carnival performer
29 Kind of daisy
30 Whirlpool

DOWN

1 Buddy of Thumper
2 Sheep seen only at night
3 Submarine detector
4 Clear picture provider
5 Air freshener brand
6 Keep out of the clutches of
7 Kudrow of "Friends"
8 Couple
9 Marks, as a ballot
15 Make high
18 Two score
19 Did nothing productive
20 Saw socially
21 Great ___ Mountains (Appalachian range)
22 Tall tale
23 Theater award
24 Latest big thing
25 ___-Magnon man

ACROSS

1 "Two Years Before the ___" (1840 account of a sailing trip)
5 First space in many board games
10 Plant used in shaving gels
11 You, for example
12 "Who's the Boss?" cougar
13 Word after special or secret
14 Stick from Australia
16 Not quite accurate
17 Appropriate
18 Part of TGIF: Abbr.
19 Boxing victories, for short
22 Schwarzenegger catchphrase, or what a 14-Across would say if it could talk
25 Goodbye, in Paris
26 Pretentious, as a film
27 React to being cut
28 Vehicle with a roll cage
29 Creator of the Lorax
30 Amount to play, in Atlantic City

DOWN

1 Cuban dance
2 Not very personable
3 What "Fitz" means in Irish names
4 Squad
5 Permanent pen
6 Yank on
7 Sunday shout
8 Pealed
9 Palindromic cable channel
15 iPod pair
18 Gets outta Dodge
19 One of the Carpenters
20 Two duos and a quartet, if they all combined
21 Talk over the computer
22 Inactive
23 In ___ of (replacing)
24 Mexican peninsula
25 "___ of Steel" (famed exercise video)

ACROSS

1 Lovable troublemakers
5 Restaurant survey name
10 Father, in France
11 Words before L.A. or Lucy
12 Actor Leslie ___ Jr. who is known for playing Aaron Burr in "Hamilton"
13 Went (over)
14 Tiny containers
16 For example
17 Wordless "yes"
18 Get a sum
19 ___-Man (eater of dots, ghosts, and power pellets)
22 Audrey Hepburn made them popular in "Roman Holiday"
25 Italian city that hosted the 2006 Winter Olympics
26 Onto
27 In the center of
28 Fish called "toro" at a sushi bar
29 They cover the forehead
30 Ready for customers

DOWN

1 Walkers often carry them
2 Magazines, TV, etc.
3 Stand-in
4 Kinda, in combinations
5 12345 or 23456
6 One way to read
7 Hiker's mix
8 Madison and Fifth, in NYC
9 Talk series whose first letter stands for "technology"
15 Last parts
18 Firing, casually
19 Build
20 Make amends (for)
21 Channel with congressional hearings
22 Mountain lion
23 Hotel room closet item
24 Roman historian who despised Julius Caesar
25 Computer key that skips ahead a few spaces

ACROSS

1 Has people over
6 Facts and figures
10 Song start
11 Neighbor of Yemen
12 The California Raisins were an example of it
14 Relatives
15 All Hallow's ___ (October 31)
16 Not over and over
18 Samuel on the Supreme Court
22 Howls
24 Roller coaster feature
25 Get with a laser gun
27 Turn blue, maybe
28 Week or two off when you don't go anywhere
32 Part of the hand
33 "Divine Comedy" poet
34 Rod under a Range Rover
35 Thrown weapon

DOWN

1 He died with what became known as a dead man's hand (two pair of aces and eights)
2 Connected to the information superhighway
3 Position
4 "Make an effort here!"
5 A handful
6 "Please continue!"
7 Friend, in Paris
8 Chinese concept
9 Woman's name that can also take an E
13 "Selma" director DuVernay
17 Certain protein
19 Element #53
20 Prius maker
21 First game in a series
23 ___ fly (play with an RBI)
26 Exaggerates, as a résumé
28 Business that may have a sensory deprivation tank
29 Money for the government
30 100%
31 Faucet

ACROSS

1 Tennis star Novak Djokovic, for example
5 Azure or aquamarine
10 Dr. Frankenstein's assistant
11 No longer snoozing
12 Unbeatable hand
14 Tiny
15 Wish you could take back
16 Swimming mammal
19 Zeus's wife (and sister)
20 Fashion lines
21 Painter who's one letter off from another painter
22 Word after cream or ginger
23 Tool with teeth
24 Disappointing finishing spot for a medal contender, and a phrase that starts and ends with the same two cards that start and end 12-Across
29 Like some movies and music
30 Website with a four-color logo
31 Doesn't eat for a while
32 Actress Russo

DOWN

1 Gentleman
2 Driving force
3 Rogers on horseback
4 Donnybrooks
5 Business named for a drink
6 Solitary bird
7 Ralph of Polo shirts
8 "Sounds good"
9 Put in the microwave
13 Majors or Daniels
16 Hypothetical start
17 Montana's capital
18 Makes changes to
19 Terrible mistake
21 Item on a den wall
23 "___ Like the Wind" (Patrick Swayze power ballad)
25 ___ for tat
26 $5 bill, in slang
27 Food container
28 Watch

ACROSS
1 List header
5 "Saturday Night ___"
10 Popular tablet
11 Kick out of the country
12 Wedding planner's fear
14 Light wood
15 Animal with whiskers
16 A few dollars short
17 Q-U connectors
19 Place for a pedicure
20 HQ
23 Make a trade
26 India's first prime minister
28 Comfortable place in the house
30 Blazing
31 Letters on invitations

32 Passed, as time
33 Gets a look at

DOWN
1 Title role for Poitier
2 Billionaire born in Kosciusko, Mississippi, familiarly
3 Seven times a week
4 Bookie's calculations
5 Brimless hat
6 Are
7 Disgusting
8 Spanish pronoun
9 "For ___?"
13 O.K. Corral surname
18 Belted out
19 Church part
20 Selected
21 Treasure-___
22 Rear ends

23 Piece of concrete
24 Coffee shop access
25 Full of enthusiasm
27 Does it wrong
29 Beatty of "Deliverance"

ACROSS

1 Brit's raincoat
4 Say no to
10 "Awesomely done!"
11 How some medicine is taken
12 Champion's time to soak up the glory
14 Bad things
15 Billy of "Titanic"
16 Tell
18 Cigs
23 Future branch
27 Operation ___ Freedom
28 What a walk-off homer scores, with the hitter doing his version of 12-Across
30 Highly decorative
31 Karaoke singer's need, for short

32 Solar ___
33 Powerful primate

DOWN

1 Shaker's companion
2 ___ and well
3 Rhodes of the Rhodes Scholarships
4 Sits up high
5 Go wrong
6 Beyonce's man
7 "___ Enchanted" (2004 film)
8 Highland family
9 Use keys
13 OMG or FTW
17 "8 Mile" actor
19 www.peta.___
20 What goes around and then comes around
21 Give gear to
22 From

23 Yahtzee category
24 Thin but strong
25 Places to crash
26 Insect that reverses to a drink
29 Suffix with Brooklyn or Akron

ACROSS

1 Hit a high point
5 Make fit, but with difficulty
10 Be a gawker
11 Clinton rival of 2008
12 Belief in many gods
14 ATM code
15 Bambi's mom, for example
16 Tooth-destroying drinks
19 Computer billionaire Michael
20 Loud landing sound
21 "Peter Pan" girl
22 One killed Cleopatra
23 Shirt-saving item
24 Bread type with many components
29 Spend lots of mirror time
30 Doing nothing
31 Male and female
32 Red cup brand

DOWN

1 Balloon sound
2 Narcissist's issue
3 "___ aboard!"
4 Phone screen feature
5 Legend in music
6 Grumpy Simpson
7 First, as a voyage
8 "Sign me up!"
9 That is to say
13 Posh word of agreement
16 Post office purchase
17 "Why not?"
18 Home for two families
19 Random trash
21 Costume store item
23 Recycling containers
25 Casual shirt
26 Hassle
27 "___ say!"
28 Prefix with conservative

ACROSS

1 Swordfight memento
5 Tycoon
10 Binge-watcher's site
11 Love, at the Louvre
12 ___ Maiden
13 Striped creature
14 Phone choice
16 Opening kickoff need
17 Serling or Stewart
18 Yik ___ (app whose second word is also the animal used as its logo)
19 ___ and haw
22 Tubular pasta
24 Having many similarities
26 Zenith
27 Against the clock
28 Viral phenomenon
29 Needing cleaning
30 Slow Churned French Silk ice cream maker

DOWN

1 J. Crew purchase
2 Double-Nobelist Marie
3 Flying solo
4 Step on a ladder
5 Shoulder-held weapon
6 Make changes to
7 Garment worn in a boxing ring
8 Not just my
9 Second Amendment org.
15 Drama category
18 "Uh-oh!"
19 Had dreams
20 Adversary
21 Talks with everyone at the party
22 Basketball hoops
23 Bring under control
24 "Would you like to check your balance?" asker
25 Tall tale

ACROSS

1 Where cranberries grow
5 A bird, or Best Actor winner Peter of "Network"
10 Real estate measurement
11 Bush successor
12 Brunch or lunch
13 Element from the Greek for "strange"
14 Game played with a shuttlecock
16 Completely irrational
17 Obies and Tonys, for example
22 Sore loser's opposite
25 Italian city where Shakespeare set "The Taming of the Shrew"
26 Large landmass
27 Fast game of chess
28 Gets torn
29 Actress/producer Witherspoon
30 John of new age music

DOWN

1 Beloved deer
2 Separator of continents
3 Alumni, casually
4 Best Picture nominee of 2014
5 Channel with many alerts
6 "Yeah, as if!"
7 Inverse of giga-
8 "It'll be fun!"
9 ___ Solo (Harrison Ford role)
15 Stunned
18 Distant
19 Amusing O'Donnell
20 Faucet issues
21 Hidden supply
22 Dorothy's last name, in "The Wizard of Oz"
23 Garfield's foil
24 There are six in an inning
25 Beer with a color in its name, for short

ACROSS

1 Bad writer
5 Anthony's costar in "The Silence of the Lambs"
10 Gusto
11 "___ you clever!"
12 Actress Dunham best known for playing Hannah Horvath
13 Such a long time
14 Cheese on a Philly cheesesteak
16 Grey's lover in "Fifty Shades of Grey"
17 Soon
22 Brigham Young University is there
25 ___ Arabians
26 Go ballistic
27 Movie musical of 1982 and 2014
28 First word of a Shakespeare title
29 Saint at the Pearly Gates
30 Gets a look at

DOWN

1 Pitches in
2 On your toes
3 Summer camp craft
4 Man without scruples
5 Comedian who's a motorcycle aficionado
6 ___ cookie balls (homemade dessert)
7 Head of a school
8 Concerning
9 Spielbergian creatures
15 Noted portrayer of Hamlet
18 Distinctive atmospheres
19 Uninspiring
20 Two-under-par hole
21 Fabiano Caruana's game
22 Glass in a door
23 Littlest of the litter
24 Grinning dog of cartoons
25 Maple syrup stuff

ACROSS

1 Six-pack stuff
5 Tablet holders
10 To a greater degree
11 Good thing
12 Dust Bowl refugee
13 Ingenuous
14 Sign put on someone's back (compare 23-Across)
16 Grass drops
17 Beta ___ (ones looking for bugs)
19 Train's end
22 Period of time
23 Words written into a dirty car's back windshield (compare 14-Across)
27 Jean jacket material
29 Sing the praises of
30 Video game company started by Nolan Bushnell
31 Kooky Sacha Baron Cohen character
32 Nice watch
33 Hurting

DOWN

1 Wild way to run
2 Norse god whose name sounds chill
3 Strumming Clapton
4 Try and, more formally
5 Williams or Redgrave
6 "This ___ travesty!"
7 To the left or right
8 One of the simple machines
9 They simmer
15 Friskies alternative
18 Electric cars
19 Tree that's the symbol of Lebanon
20 "In sooth, you ___ blame": Desdemona
21 Everyday
24 Golden ring
25 Sierra Club founder John
26 Precipice
28 Strong anger

ACROSS

1 ___-Irish
6 God played by Anthony Hopkins in 2011
10 "Go this way" indicator
11 Sound system name
12 Pacific island group whose capital is Apia
13 Got bigger
14 Ben E. King's signature song
16 Currency for Kurosawa
17 Comfy room
18 One of its letters stands for "loving"
19 Pts. of the Bible
22 "Make yourself comfortable!"
25 Nuggets of wisdom
26 Extremely
27 Tag information
28 Thai appetizer
29 Prepare a revolution
30 Numbers like 8 and 88

DOWN

1 Like some teenagers
2 Shipping container
3 Suze with financial views
4 Many a "Who Framed Roger Rabbit" character
5 Wrap, as a newborn
6 Doc for women only
7 U. building
8 "Fascinating ..."
9 Fresh
15 Wry reply to "Why?"
18 Show shower
19 Entertainer Midler
20 Donna of DKNY
21 Sticks around
22 Get better
23 Guns & ___ (magazine about magazines)
24 Czech or Slovak, say
25 Economics stat

ACROSS

1 Cries one's eyes out
5 Feeds, as hogs
10 "That was a close one!"
11 Gandhi contemporary
12 Having the power
13 Bagel variety
14 Singer Parton's theme park in Pigeon Forge, Tennessee
16 Peeper shutter
17 Home to many a SoCal resident
22 India's movie industry
25 Moved the dinghy
26 In the center of
27 "___ we going to be late?"
28 Hardly worth mentioning
29 Sauce made from pine nuts
30 Fisherman's spot

DOWN

1 One of thirteen in a deck of cards
2 Exasperated phrase
3 Lovely lady
4 "Awesome!" back in the day
5 Student's mini-vacation
6 Jokey Jay
7 John Glenn's state
8 Cattle ___
9 Free source of light
15 Let go first
18 Overwhelm
19 Marisa in a "Seinfeld" episode
20 French river known for its beautiful valley
21 Snake that sounds like a math expert
22 Dull person
23 Has to pay back
24 40-day period
25 Wiz Khalifa's musical genre

ACROSS

1 Gulf
6 Web browser button
10 Lacking proper authority
11 Calculating Turing
12 "___ see!"
13 Elmer's stuff
14 Dog breed named for the capital of China
16 Agree
17 Rift, as in a friendship
21 Dog breed named for the capital of Tibet
25 "My Name Is ___"
26 Trapezoid or triangle
28 Clue weapon made of lead
29 Wristwatch brand
30 Turkey ___ (common name for a running race held on Thanksgiving)
31 Put into office

DOWN

1 Bawl
2 Basketball rim
3 Feverish shivering
4 Stew in your own juices
5 Mellifluous Manchester
6 Like some pants
7 Where strikes and spares are scored
8 ___ and effect
9 Bending pair
15 Hindi greeting heard in yoga class
17 Snoozed
18 Four-legged thing
19 Oprah Winfrey's production company
20 Possibly uninhabited piece of land
22 "Invisible Touch" singer Collins
23 "Ditto"
24 Its first letter does not stand for "oil"
27 Part of some tel. nos.

ACROSS

1 Transcriber of Holmes's adventures
7 Sometimes called
10 Christie of mystery
11 It's good for the French
12 Wealthy European country
14 Cafe au ___
15 Maine college
16 Watched someone's cats, say
17 Wasn't renewed, as a subscription
21 Pleasant news for the nose
22 Exchange
26 What you see a lot of in 12-Across
28 Presidential first name
29 Walt Whitman's "___ of Grass"
30 Used to be
31 Least loopy

DOWN

1 Pink Floyd album, with "The"
2 Water, in Oaxaca
3 Uber car, more or less
4 "Keep it as it is," to a proofreader
5 Unit of resistance
6 Collared, as a crook
7 Shares a border with
8 Divided peninsula
9 Worry
13 Cereal grain
16 Beautiful string
17 Drama with Susan Dey and Corbin Bernsen
18 Caribbean vacation spot
19 Plagues
20 Sch. that hosts the George W. Bush Presidential Library and Museum
22 Look over
23 Tidal ___
24 God of war
25 "Hey, buddy! Over here!"
27 Vote for

ACROSS

1 Second letter
5 Having seen it all, and not too impressed
10 In good shape
11 With 27-Down, Caprese salad topper
12 Phrase that means "cause great disorder"
14 Pink wine, briefly
15 Finnish entrée
16 Tried to be faster than the others
19 Donate
20 They may clash
21 Like a buff person's muscles
22 Many college degs.
23 "Bosom Buddies" buddy
24 Phrase that means "great disorder"
29 Pants material
30 Illuminated theater sign
31 Alleviates
32 Count (on)

DOWN

1 "Incidentally," in three letters
2 Do it wrong
3 Piece of business attire
4 Leaves thunderstruck
5 Candy or Coltrane
6 In the style of
7 Get right to it
8 Become better over time
9 Punched out
13 Joke around
16 "You shouldn't have done that!" is one
17 Award for mystery writers
18 Sportscaster Bob
19 Minnesota resident, casually
21 Spasm
23 "American Idol" winner Allen
25 ___ out a living
26 Swung tool
27 See 11-Across
28 Hog home

1	2	3	4		5	6	7	8	9
10					11				
12				13					
			14				15		
16	17	18				19			
20					21				
22				23					
24			25			26	27	28	
29					30				
31					32				

ACROSS

1 Irritates
5 Baltimore team before the Ravens
10 Richmond-born tennis champ
11 Regarding
12 Gas used in Las Vegas
13 Bradshaw or Gross
14 "Not to make a big deal out of it, though"
16 Choose
17 "If you would," when texting
18 Nixon met with him in China
19 TV show with a spinoff set in Miami
22 North Korea's capital
25 For all to hear
26 Spoken

27 Remote control button
28 Full of energy
29 Kitchenware glass
30 Too

DOWN

1 Guitar's cousin
2 Consume, as resources
3 One of four in Pac-Man
4 Emailed
5 Junk mail, often
6 Does as commanded
7 Actress Petty
8 Become sour
9 Home with hay
15 Aerobics class material
18 Little cheese lover
19 December song
20 Problems

21 Thermos brand
22 iPod button
23 Elton John's "___ Song"
24 Mat activity
25 Droid download

1	2	3	4		5	6	7	8	9
10					11				
12					13				
14				15					
16				17					
			18				19	20	21
	22	23			24				
25					26				
27					28				
29					30				

ACROSS

1 Tire problem
5 Unexpected plot action
10 Unclothed
11 Sought aid from
12 Be so happy
14 Palindromic king
15 One, to Italians
16 Slew
19 Lose sleep
20 Sixth anniversary gift
21 ___ double take (reacts, maybe)
22 Feeling down
23 Chum
24 So happy
29 Fully consume
30 October's birthstone
31 Annoying people
32 Despicable person

DOWN

1 Presidential nickname that's also a basketball nickname
2 Water, to Jacques Cousteau
3 One of a bodily pair
4 Didn't say
5 Homer gait
6 Simple card game
7 Cause harm to
8 Mancala pieces
9 Tundra and Sequoia maker
13 A good time
16 Serve, as food
17 Poker announcement
18 Evades
19 Twitter command
21 Novelist Brown
23 Daddy
25 Pizza ___
26 Wall St. event
27 A long way
28 Common tree

1	2	3	4	■	5	6	7	8	9
10					11				
12				13					
■			14			■	15		
16	17	18			■	19			
20				■	21				
22			■	23			■	■	■
24			25			26	27	28	
29				■	30				
31				■	32				

ACROSS

1 Animals common in Mongolia
5 African language group
10 Help, as criminals
11 Seize, as power
12 Coffee shop order
13 Seattle or Los Angeles newspaper
14 Presidential nickname
16 Has faith in
17 On the way up
22 Another presidential nickname
25 Nobel Prize winner born Maria Sklodowska
26 Helper
27 Airborne
28 Blood carrier
29 Advance-the-runner ploys
30 Makes a blunder

DOWN

1 Fun boat
2 More than dislike
3 Reeves of "Speed"
4 Pens
5 Gives unwanted advice
6 Atlas section
7 Anesthetized
8 Poplar or pine
9 Company with brown trucks
15 Main and 1st
18 Fight (off)
19 Less friendly
20 Low point
21 Scottish valleys
22 George Takei role
23 Its chemical symbol is Fe
24 Raise
25 Hack's vehicle

4

S	A	L	K	■	F	A	U	N	A
A	M	I	N	■	L	I	N	E	N
J	A	N	E	A	U	S	T	E	N
A	Z	T	E	C	■	L	O	D	E
K	E	Y	■	L	E	E	■	■	
■	■	H	U	T	■	A	S	S	
A	S	T	O	■	T	A	S	T	E
J	O	H	N	H	U	S	T	O	N
A	S	I	D	E	■	A	R	O	D
X	A	N	A	X	■	P	O	P	S

5

A	D	O	R	E	D	■	A	M	P
C	U	P	O	L	A	■	L	A	O
R	E	A	D	M	Y	L	I	P	S
E	L	L	E	■	T	A	B	L	E
■	■	■	■	C	O	P	I	E	S
E	D	I	S	O	N	■	■	■	
X	E	N	O	N	■	B	D	A	Y
T	W	I	S	T	M	Y	A	R	M
R	E	C	■	A	T	O	M	I	C
A	Y	E	■	C	A	B	E	Z	A

6

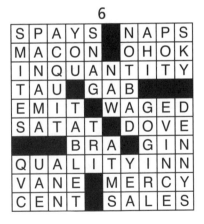

S	P	A	Y	S	■	N	A	P	S
M	A	C	O	N	■	O	H	O	K
I	N	Q	U	A	N	T	I	T	Y
T	A	U	■	G	A	B	■		
E	M	I	T	■	W	A	G	E	D
S	A	T	A	T	■	D	O	V	E
■	■	B	R	A	■	G	I	N	
Q	U	A	L	I	T	Y	I	N	N
V	A	N	E	■	M	E	R	C	Y
C	E	N	T	■	S	A	L	E	S

7

J	I	V	E	■	B	R	I	A	N
O	V	A	L	■	R	A	D	I	O
C	A	L	M	W	A	T	E	R	S
K	N	I	S	H	■	E	A	S	Y
S	A	D	■	I	T	D	■		
■	■	S	P	A	■	B	A	H	
S	P	O	T	■	I	T	A	L	Y
L	A	K	E	P	L	A	C	I	D
A	G	R	E	E	■	D	O	E	R
Y	E	A	R	N	■	A	N	N	A

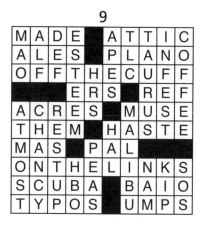

Puzzle 8:

B	A	C	H	■	S	T	O	K	E
A	W	A	Y	■	H	A	D	I	N
N	A	P	A	■	A	X	I	N	G
D	I	R	T	Y	M	I	N	D	■
S	T	A	T	U	E	■	■	■	■
■	■	■	K	O	S	H	E	R	
■	B	R	A	I	N	W	A	S	H
A	R	E	N	T	■	A	L	S	O
H	A	I	K	U	■	P	L	E	D
A	S	N	A	P	■	S	E	X	Y

Puzzle 9:

M	A	D	E	■	A	T	T	I	C
A	L	E	S	■	P	L	A	N	O
O	F	F	T	H	E	C	U	F	F
■	■	■	E	R	S	■	R	E	F
A	C	R	E	S	■	M	U	S	E
T	H	E	M	■	H	A	S	T	E
M	A	S	■	P	A	L	■	■	
O	N	T	H	E	L	I	N	K	S
S	C	U	B	A	■	B	A	I	O
T	Y	P	O	S	■	U	M	P	S

Puzzle 10:

B	A	T	T	E	D	■	Y	E	T
O	T	O	O	L	E	■	O	V	A
C	O	R	N	Y	J	O	K	E	S
A	N	N	E	■	A	R	E	N	T
■	■	■	S	V	E	L	T	E	
N	A	S	S	A	U	■	■	■	
A	L	I	E	N	■	O	R	E	O
C	O	M	E	D	Y	G	O	L	D
H	U	P	■	R	E	L	A	I	D
O	D	S	■	A	R	E	N	A	S

Puzzle 11:

P	A	I	R	■	R	E	B	U	S
A	X	L	E	■	A	G	E	N	T
D	E	L	T	A	F	O	R	C	E
■	■	A	R	T	■	L	O	L	
S	H	E	I	K	■	G	I	R	L
T	A	L	L	■	T	O	N	K	A
E	R	A	■	P	O	E	■	■	
A	L	P	H	A	M	A	L	E	S
L	O	S	E	R	■	S	O	L	O
S	W	E	D	E	■	Y	U	K	S

12

K	A	L	■	C	A	B	B	I	E
O	D	E	■	A	N	A	L	O	G
D	O	N	K	E	Y	K	O	N	G
A	R	I	E	S	■	E	B	A	Y
K	E	N	Y	A	N	■			
■			R	A	T	E	D	G	
A	R	I	A	■	V	A	L	O	R
D	O	N	Q	U	I	X	O	T	E
A	S	S	U	R	E	■	P	E	A
M	E	T	A	L	S	■	E	S	T

13

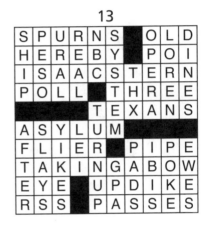

S	P	U	R	N	S	■	O	L	D
H	E	R	E	B	Y	■	P	O	I
I	S	A	A	C	S	T	E	R	N
P	O	L	L	■	T	H	R	E	E
■				T	E	X	A	N	S
A	S	Y	L	U	M	■			
F	L	I	E	R	■	P	I	P	E
T	A	K	I	N	G	A	B	O	W
E	Y	E	■	U	P	D	I	K	E
R	S	S	■	P	A	S	S	E	S

14

N	U	D	G	E	D	■	S	P	A
S	T	E	L	L	A	■	W	A	R
F	A	K	E	F	R	I	E	N	D
W	H	E	E	■	E	V	A	D	E
■			A	M	Y	T	A	N	■
A	B	L	A	Z	E	■			
F	O	I	S	T	■	B	R	O	S
F	A	L	S	E	F	R	O	N	T
I	S	A	■	C	L	A	N	C	Y
X	T	C	■	S	U	S	S	E	X

15

L	A	O	S	■	P	A	U	S	E
B	L	A	H	■	E	S	S	E	X
J	F	K	A	I	R	P	O	R	T
■			M	R	T	■	P	E	R
C	O	P	E	S	■	L	E	N	A
O	U	I	S	■	T	I	N	A	S
E	T	C	■	S	E	E	■		
R	F	K	S	T	A	D	I	U	M
C	O	U	P	E	■	T	A	S	E
E	X	P	A	T	■	O	M	A	N

16

F	L	A	Y	■	D	I	S	K	S
D	A	D	A	■	O	C	T	E	T
R	O	O	K	I	E	Y	E	A	R
■	■	K	O	S	■	E	T	A	
D	U	D	E	S	■	B	L	O	T
I	P	O	D	■	B	U	E	N	A
O	N	O	■	H	E	R	■	■	
D	E	B	U	T	A	L	B	U	M
E	X	I	S	T	■	A	R	E	A
S	T	E	E	P	■	P	A	Y	S

17

M	G	M	■	D	E	N	I	R	O
E	R	A	■	A	G	E	G	A	P
L	E	M	O	N	G	R	O	V	E
D	E	B	U	G	■	F	R	E	D
S	K	A	T	E	S	■	■	■	
■	■	■	R	U	B	B	E	R	
C	A	G	E	■	G	U	A	V	A
U	S	E	D	C	A	R	L	O	T
B	A	N	G	O	R	■	E	K	E
S	P	E	E	D	Y	■	D	E	S

18

S	H	E	E	N	A	■	T	A	D
C	O	A	X	E	S	■	U	N	I
T	H	R	E	E	K	I	N	G	S
V	O	L	S	■	F	R	I	S	K
■	■	■	B	O	A	S	T	S	
N	A	S	C	A	R	■	■	■	
O	R	E	O	S	■	D	R	O	P
F	O	U	R	Q	U	E	E	N	S
A	M	S	■	U	R	A	N	U	S
T	A	S	■	E	L	D	E	S	T

19

B	O	P	■	D	A	Y	T	O	N
A	B	E	■	A	D	M	I	R	E
L	A	N	D	L	O	C	K	E	D
E	M	A	I	L	■	A	I	M	S
S	A	L	M	A	N	■	■	■	
■	■	■	■	S	I	G	N	I	N
S	P	I	T	■	G	U	A	V	A
K	A	Z	A	K	H	S	T	A	N
I	G	O	T	I	T	■	A	N	N
S	E	D	A	N	S	■	L	A	Y

20

```
E D I T █ C H O S E
A U D I █ R U N O N
T H I N K A H E A D
█ █ █ M O M █ I K E
S P C A S █ S L U R
E L O N █ G U L P S
E E L █ A R C █ █ █
F A L L B E H I N D
I S A A C █ A C H E
T E R P S █ S E L L
```

21

```
F R A Y █ B A S A L
R O T E █ U S A G E
O D E S █ L I N E D
D I A N E L A D D █
O N T O U R █ █ █ █
█ █ █ █ R U S S I A
█ J A S O N K I D D
R U N U P █ A X E D
A S T R O █ T E A T
S T E E P █ E S S O
```

22

```
G A T E █ A C U T E
E A R N █ B O R A X
C H E V Y C H A S E
K E N Y A █ E L K S
O D D █ D E N █ █ █
█ █ █ L A P █ G O P
S O L E █ I G L O O
C H E V Y C R U Z E
A N G I E █ I T E M
R O O S T █ M E S S
```

23

```
S T A T █ D A R E S
T O G O █ E X I L E
I R A N █ B E G A T
L A Z Y S U S A N █
T H E S E S █ █ █ █
█ █ █ █ I S L E T S
█ C R A Z Y I V A N
S U E M E █ C O K E
P R I M O █ I K E A
A D D O N █ T E N D
```

24

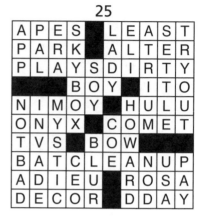

R	S	S		V	E	R	B	A	L
E	C	U		I	G	U	A	N	A
B	A	N	K	R	O	B	B	E	R
U	N	R	I	G		S	E	W	S
S	T	A	T	I	C				
				L	L	A	M	A	S
A	Q	U	A		O	P	A	R	T
B	U	R	N	R	U	B	B	E	R
B	I	G	K	I	D		E	N	E
A	T	E	A	M	S		L	A	P

25

A	P	E	S		L	E	A	S	T
P	A	R	K		A	L	T	E	R
P	L	A	Y	S	D	I	R	T	Y
			B	O	Y		I	T	O
N	I	M	O	Y		H	U	L	U
O	N	Y	X		C	O	M	E	T
T	V	S		B	O	W			
B	A	T	C	L	E	A	N	U	P
A	D	I	E	U		R	O	S	A
D	E	C	O	R		D	D	A	Y

26

C	A	L	M		T	A	B	B	Y
O	P	E	C		E	X	I	L	E
B	U	I	C	K	R	E	G	A	L
			A	I	M		M	I	L
B	A	S	I	N		D	A	N	A
I	R	O	N		F	A	C	E	T
S	O	D		I	A	N			
Q	U	I	C	K	R	I	G	H	T
U	N	D	U	E		S	O	M	E
E	D	I	T	S		H	O	M	E

27

S	L	I	P	U	P		P	H	D
E	U	R	O	P	A		I	O	U
C	L	A	S	S	C	L	O	W	N
T	U	N	E		M	O	U	S	E
				L	A	S	S	O	S
W	O	O	D	E	N				
A	S	C	O	T		A	R	T	S
S	C	H	O	O	L	F	O	O	L
T	A	R		F	O	R	O	N	E
E	R	E		F	O	O	T	E	D

28

```
T E N T H S ■ L E D
O V E R I T ■ E V A
T A X I D R I V E R
O N T O ■ A R E N T
■ ■ ■ C I A L I S
I N T E R N ■
N E H R U ■ K O B E
F A R E M I N D E D
U T E ■ B O E I N G
N O W ■ S N E E Z Y
```

29

```
P O N Z I ■ C H A P
O R I O N ■ R A G E
W I N E C O O L E R
D O J ■ A R C ■
E L A N ■ B U R G S
R E S E T ■ S O R E
■ W O K ■ O I C
H A N D W A R M E R
A S I A ■ N A I V E
W A X Y ■ T W E E T
```

30

```
L O B ■ S E R I A L
I C E ■ A G E N D A
S T R A I G H T A S
P E R I L ■ M O M S
S T A R E S ■
■ D O S A G E
S H E A ■ V E N I N
C A T C H I N G Z S
A R C H I E ■ E M U
B E H E S T ■ R O E
```

31

```
G A P ■ P H O E B E
E M O ■ H A N D E L
T B O N E S T E A K
A L L A N ■ O N U S
B E S T O F ■
■ M R M O T O
S A M E ■ E A S E L
T B A L L S T A N D
O B R I E N ■ K O I
P A S S G O ■ A R E
```

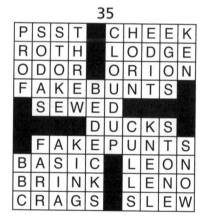

32

33

34

35

36

B	R	A	S	■	G	O	B	A	D
D	E	L	I	■	A	R	O	M	A
A	B	I	T	■	N	E	W	I	N
Y	U	K	O	N	G	O	L	D	■
S	T	E	N	O	S	■	■	■	■
■	■	■	S	T	A	S	I	S	
■	Y	O	U	C	A	N	T	G	O
N	O	T	S	O	■	N	O	E	L
O	U	T	E	R	■	O	N	T	O
P	R	O	S	E	■	Y	E	A	S

37

P	I	L	A	F	■	P	A	T	S
I	N	U	S	E	■	A	T	I	T
E	E	R	I	E	■	D	A	T	A
■	Z	E	A	L	O	U	S	L	Y
■	■	■	S	N	A	K	E	S	
E	N	C	A	S	E	■	■	■	
J	E	A	L	O	U	S	L	Y	■
E	V	I	L	■	P	I	P	E	R
C	E	R	A	■	O	R	G	A	N
T	R	O	Y	■	N	E	A	R	S

38

S	N	O	R	T	S	■	M	L	S
H	O	H	O	H	O	■	O	U	I
A	N	N	I	E	S	S	O	N	G
W	O	O	L	■	O	P	R	A	H
■	■	■	F	O	Y	E	R	S	
S	A	T	U	R	N	■	■	■	
C	R	A	Z	E	■	C	O	E	N
A	R	N	I	E	S	A	R	M	Y
N	O	G	■	L	U	R	E	I	N
T	W	O	■	Y	E	A	S	T	Y

39

P	A	C	■	C	A	P	G	U	N
A	B	U	■	I	G	U	A	N	A
L	O	B	S	T	E	R	B	I	B
E	V	E	R	I	■	L	E	T	S
R	E	D	I	N	K	■	■	■	
■	■	■	G	I	A	N	T	S	
A	C	L	U	■	C	H	A	R	O
S	H	I	S	H	K	A	B	O	B
K	A	R	E	E	M	■	O	V	A
S	P	A	R	S	E	■	B	E	D

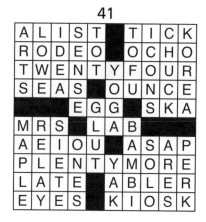

H	E	L	P	█	K	A	R	M	A
A	L	O	E	█	F	R	E	E	S
F	I	F	T	Y	C	E	N	T	S
T	O	T	E	M	█	N	E	A	T
S	T	Y	█	C	O	T	█	█	█
█	█	O	A	T	█	M	I	T	█
C	H	E	F	█	T	E	A	C	H
H	A	L	F	D	O	L	L	A	R
E	L	M	E	R	█	M	I	L	E
M	O	O	R	S	█	S	A	L	E

A	L	I	S	T	█	T	I	C	K
R	O	D	E	O	█	O	C	H	O
T	W	E	N	T	Y	F	O	U	R
S	E	A	S	█	O	U	N	C	E
█	█	█	E	G	G	█	S	K	A
M	R	S	█	L	A	B	█	█	█
A	E	I	O	U	█	A	S	A	P
P	L	E	N	T	Y	M	O	R	E
L	A	T	E	█	A	B	L	E	R
E	Y	E	S	█	K	I	O	S	K

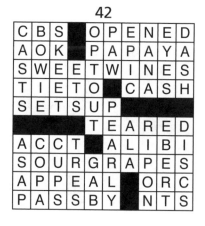

C	B	S	█	O	P	E	N	E	D
A	O	K	█	P	A	P	A	Y	A
S	W	E	E	T	W	I	N	E	S
T	I	E	T	O	█	C	A	S	H
S	E	T	S	U	P	█	█	█	█
█	█	█	T	E	A	R	E	D	
A	C	C	T	█	A	L	I	B	I
S	O	U	R	G	R	A	P	E	S
A	P	P	E	A	L	█	O	R	C
P	A	S	S	B	Y	█	N	T	S

U	T	A	H	A	N	█	A	R	T
M	O	B	I	L	E	█	W	A	R
P	U	B	L	I	C	F	A	C	E
S	T	A	T	█	K	O	R	E	A
█	█	█	█	M	E	R	E	S	T
S	C	A	R	E	D	█	█	█	█
T	A	X	E	D	█	D	R	A	W
P	R	I	V	A	T	E	E	Y	E
A	G	O	█	L	O	A	N	E	D
T	O	M	█	S	T	R	E	S	S

44

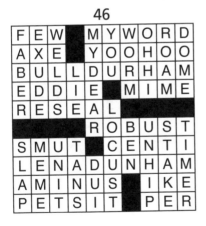

```
L A P ■ W R I T E R
A K A ■ H O P E T O
B I L L Y B A R T Y
O R I O N ■ D I E S
R A N L O W ■ ■ ■
■ ■ ■ T A P T A P
E L S E ■ H O U S E
W I L L Y W O N K A
A Z A L E A ■ A I R
N A M A T H ■ S N L
```

45

```
S C A R ■ B A R O N
H U L U ■ A M O U R
I R O N ■ Z E B R A
R I N G T O N E ■
T E E ■ R O D ■ ■
■ Y A K ■ H E M
■ R I G A T O N I
A L I K E ■ A P E X
T I M E D ■ M E M E
M E S S Y ■ E D Y S
```

46

```
F E W ■ M Y W O R D
A X E ■ Y O O H O O
B U L L D U R H A M
E D D I E ■ M I M E
R E S E A L ■ ■
■ ■ R O B U S T
S M U T ■ C E N T I
L E N A D U N H A M
A M I N U S ■ I K E
P E T S I T ■ P E R
```

47

```
N E M O ■ W A N D A
I W O N ■ I B E A M
N O O N ■ L O O N Y
J K R O W L I N G
A S S ■ O I L ■
■ T E A ■ S K I
■ J K S I M M O N S
P E A K S ■ A L E S
S A L E M ■ L I E U
S N I D E ■ I D L E
```

48

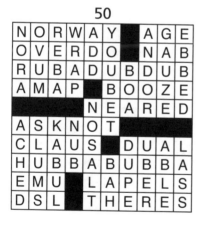

49

50

51

52

```
S C R A M ■ E D A M
P R I N E ■ C O L A
H I L T O N H E A D
E M I ■ W O O ■ ■ ■
R E N T ■ T E N A M
E A G E R ■ S O F A
■ ■ R A P ■ D R Y ■
H A M M E R H E A D
O B O E ■ O B A M A
W E E D ■ F O L E Y
```

53

```
F A N G ■ M E M O S
O V E R ■ E G Y P T
R A D I O T O W E R
■ ■ S K A ■ O N O ■
T E L L S ■ T R E K
H U E Y ■ M A D R E
I R A ■ J A Y ■ ■ ■
R O D E O C L O W N
S P I N E ■ O H I O
T E N D S ■ R O I D
```

54

```
M A L I B U ■ H I M
A M A Z O N ■ A D O
M O Z Z A R E L L A
A K E Y ■ E L L E N
■ ■ ■ F A K E R S ■
S E W E L L ■ ■ ■ ■
A M I G O ■ C L A Y
G O R G O N Z O L A
A T E ■ R E A G A N
N E D ■ S T R O N G
```

55

```
H I S S E D ■ S A L
A V A T A R ■ P R O
W A T E R P R O O F
K N E W ■ H E I S T
■ ■ ■ A I S L E S ■
A P P A L L ■ ■ ■ ■
S H A R P ■ F E T A
H I T T H E R O O F
E S S ■ A V E N G E
S H Y ■ S E E S A W
```

S	A	G	A	S	■	C	R	O	P
Q	U	E	S	T	■	H	E	R	E
U	P	T	H	E	R	I	V	E	R
A	A	S	■	M	O	P	■	■	
R	I	T	A	■	D	I	D	I	T
E	R	O	D	E	■	N	O	S	H
■	■	O	D	E	■	T	R	U	
D	O	W	N	S	T	R	E	A	M
A	N	T	I	■	C	E	L	E	B
M	E	S	S	■	H	I	L	L	S

P	A	L	E	O	■	Y	I	P	S
A	L	I	B	I	■	O	K	R	A
T	U	M	B	L	E	W	E	E	D
I	M	P	■	Y	A	Z	■	■	
O	N	E	S	■	R	A	L	P	H
S	I	D	E	A	■	H	O	H	O
■	■	A	L	F	■	V	O	W	
B	U	M	B	L	E	B	E	E	S
I	S	E	E	■	L	E	T	B	E
B	A	N	D	■	L	A	T	E	R

S	A	R	I	■	S	U	P	E	R
T	E	E	M	■	O	S	A	K	A
I	S	L	E	■	F	A	C	E	D
R	O	A	D	R	A	G	E	■	
S	P	Y	■	A	B	E	■	■	
■	■	O	D	E	■	M	A	P	
■	R	O	I	D	R	A	G	E	
P	L	A	Z	A	■	E	U	R	O
R	A	V	E	N	■	E	V	E	N
E	X	I	S	T	■	F	E	E	S

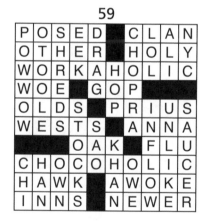

P	O	S	E	D	■	C	L	A	N
O	T	H	E	R	■	H	O	L	Y
W	O	R	K	A	H	O	L	I	C
W	O	E	■	G	O	P	■	■	
O	L	D	S	■	P	R	I	U	S
W	E	S	T	S	■	A	N	N	A
■	■	O	A	K	■	F	L	U	
C	H	O	C	O	H	O	L	I	C
H	A	W	K	■	A	W	O	K	E
I	N	N	S	■	N	E	W	E	R

60

F	A	S	T	■	O	T	T	E	R
A	L	T	O	■	A	B	O	V	E
N	O	R	T	H	K	O	R	E	A
C	H	A	S	E	■	N	E	R	D
Y	A	Y	■	L	E	E	■		
		G	P	A	■	R	O	D	
U	P	D	O	■	R	H	Y	M	E
S	O	U	T	H	S	U	D	A	N
S	L	A	T	E	■	N	E	H	I
R	E	L	A	Y	■	G	R	A	M

61

B	A	A	■	C	H	O	M	P	S
E	L	M	■	H	A	N	D	E	L
G	P	A	■	I	L	L	S	A	Y
G	A	Z	E	L	L	E	■		
E	C	O	L	I	■	A	L	A	S
D	A	N	E	■	A	V	E	R	T
			G	A	Z	E	T	T	E
R	E	C	A	N	T	■	S	U	V
B	R	O	N	T	E	■	I	R	E
S	E	P	T	I	C	■	N	O	N

62

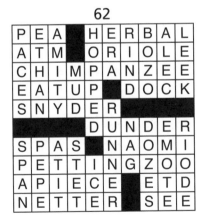

P	E	A	■	H	E	R	B	A	L
A	T	M	■	O	R	I	O	L	E
C	H	I	M	P	A	N	Z	E	E
E	A	T	U	P	■	D	O	C	K
S	N	Y	D	E	R	■			
		D	U	N	D	E	R		
S	P	A	S	■	N	A	O	M	I
P	E	T	T	I	N	G	Z	O	O
A	P	I	E	C	E	■	E	T	D
N	E	T	T	E	R	■	S	E	E

63

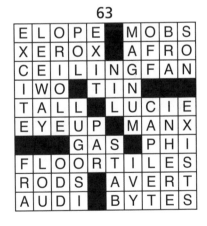

E	L	O	P	E	■	M	O	B	S
X	E	R	O	X	■	A	F	R	O
C	E	I	L	I	N	G	F	A	N
I	W	O	■	T	I	N	■		
T	A	L	L	■	L	U	C	I	E
E	Y	E	U	P	■	M	A	N	X
		G	A	S	■	P	H	I	
F	L	O	O	R	T	I	L	E	S
R	O	D	S	■	A	V	E	R	T
A	U	D	I	■	B	Y	T	E	S

64

R	A	M	P	S		D	O	E	S
A	R	I	S	E		E	L	M	O
F	A	M	I	L	Y	F	E	U	D
F	B	I		F	E	E			
L	I	N	T		T	A	P	E	S
E	A	G	E	R		T	R	U	E
			R	E	P		E	R	A
F	E	A	R	F	A	C	T	O	R
E	R	G	O		S	H	A	P	E
D	E	E	R		S	E	X	E	D

65

T	H	A	I		S	A	A	B	S
B	O	R	G		A	S	T	R	O
T	W	E	L	F	T	H	M	A	N
			O	D	E		F	I	N
G	A	T	O	R		C	E	D	E
O	T	I	S		W	I	E	S	T
T	H	E			I	A	N		
F	O	U	R	T	H	D	O	W	N
I	M	P	E	I		E	R	I	E
T	E	S	T	S		R	E	N	T

66

B	A	S	K	I	N		C	S	A
A	C	T	I	V	E		L	O	U
C	H	E	S	S	B	O	A	R	D
H	E	M	S		U	N	I	T	E
				A	L	T	M	A	N
R	E	D	S	E	A				
E	R	I	K	S		L	U	T	E
C	R	A	Y	O	L	A	B	O	X
A	O	L		P	I	L	E	U	P
P	R	S		S	B	A	R	R	O

67

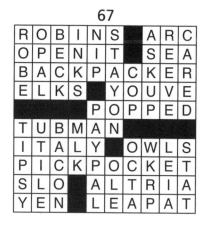

R	O	B	I	N	S		A	R	C
O	P	E	N	I	T		S	E	A
B	A	C	K	P	A	C	K	E	R
E	L	K	S		Y	O	U	V	E
					P	O	P	P	E	D
T	U	B	M	A	N				
I	T	A	L	Y		O	W	L	S
P	I	C	K	P	O	C	K	E	T
S	L	O		A	L	T	R	I	A
Y	E	N		L	E	A	P	A	T

68

J	A	M	B	■	C	I	S	C	O
A	S	I	A	■	A	L	L	A	N
R	A	C	K	O	F	L	A	M	B
■	■	E	W	E	■	P	E	A	
T	I	E	R	S	■	B	O	O	S
I	N	D	Y	■	D	E	N	S	E
P	S	I	■	I	O	U	■	■	■
O	U	T	O	N	A	L	I	M	B
F	R	O	W	N	■	A	R	E	A
F	E	R	N	S	■	H	E	L	D

69

A	P	A	C	E	■	E	R	I	C
C	O	V	E	N	■	Y	O	K	O
T	W	E	E	D	L	E	D	E	E
O	W	N	■	S	O	L	■	■	
R	O	U	T	■	L	I	B	E	L
S	W	E	A	T	■	D	E	M	I
■	■	■	M	U	G	■	K	E	N
T	W	E	E	T	Y	B	I	R	D
E	A	R	L	■	R	A	N	G	E
X	R	A	Y	■	O	G	D	E	N

70

B	O	R	A	T	■	C	A	S	K
I	N	A	N	E	■	O	H	I	O
G	L	I	T	T	E	R	A	T	I
M	I	L	■	E	V	E	■	■	■
A	N	E	W	■	A	R	B	O	R
C	E	D	A	R	■	S	O	R	E
■	■	■	S	U	B	■	N	A	M
T	W	I	T	T	E	R	A	T	I
W	A	K	E	■	S	I	M	O	N
A	Y	E	S	■	T	B	I	R	D

71

S	P	U	D	S	■	A	B	B	A
H	A	S	U	P	■	T	O	L	L
A	L	O	H	A	S	T	A	T	E
Z	A	P	■	M	I	A	■	■	■
A	C	E	S	■	S	C	R	A	M
M	E	N	U	S	■	K	E	N	O
■	■	■	C	E	O	■	E	A	R
A	L	P	H	A	V	I	L	L	E
H	A	H	A	■	A	D	I	O	S
A	D	D	S	■	L	O	N	G	O

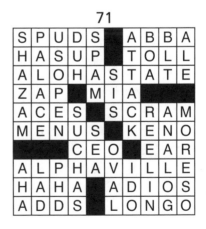

T	E	D	█	L	E	T	H	A	L
E	R	A	█	A	T	H	E	N	A
B	I	N	G	O	C	A	R	D	S
O	C	T	E	T	█	T	O	Y	S
W	H	E	E	Z	E	█	█	█	█
█	█	█	█	U	R	B	A	N	A
C	L	O	T	█	A	L	T	E	R
R	I	N	G	O	S	T	A	R	R
I	N	L	I	N	E	█	L	V	I
P	A	Y	F	O	R	█	L	E	D

A	T	M	S	█	█	G	I	G	I
U	H	O	H	█	P	O	W	E	R
R	I	P	A	█	R	O	O	M	S
A	C	E	Q	U	E	E	N	█	█
S	K	Y	█	P	R	Y	█	█	█
█	█	█	S	H	E	█	J	F	K
█	I	C	E	Q	U	E	E	N	█
C	A	R	O	L	█	P	A	N	E
B	L	A	N	D	█	O	N	C	E
S	A	N	E	█	█	N	E	E	D

B	O	N	D	S	█	S	O	F	A
A	B	O	U	T	█	E	W	A	N
A	R	T	H	U	R	P	E	N	N
B	I	B	█	B	U	T	█	█	█
A	A	A	H	█	B	I	R	C	H
A	N	D	E	S	█	C	O	L	A
█	█	█	█	C	A	P	█	L	E	T
B	A	N	K	T	E	L	L	E	R
B	A	I	L	█	R	O	U	S	E
C	A	P	E	█	U	P	P	E	D

W	A	S	N	T	█	R	A	U	L
A	L	P	H	A	█	E	X	P	O
I	B	E	L	I	E	V	E	S	O
T	A	N	█	L	A	S	█	█	█
E	N	D	S	█	T	U	N	A	S
D	Y	S	O	N	█	P	O	L	K
█	█	█	█	M	A	C	█	S	E	A
I	D	O	U	B	T	T	H	A	T
S	Y	N	C	█	R	E	E	S	E
M	E	S	H	█	L	A	S	T	S

76

W	I	D	E	N	■	L	O	I	S
A	C	U	R	A	■	A	U	D	I
S	E	P	A	R	A	T	I	O	N
H	B	O	■	C	O	T	■	■	■
M	O	N	T	■	L	E	A	N	S
E	X	T	R	A	■	S	C	O	T
■	■	■	U	N	O	■	A	C	E
K	E	V	I	N	B	A	C	O	N
I	T	I	S	■	E	X	I	S	T
M	A	A	M	■	Y	E	A	T	S

77

W	A	F	E	R	■	S	T	E	W
E	V	I	T	A	■	O	H	S	O
B	E	N	A	F	F	L	E	C	K
C	N	N	■	T	B	A	■	■	■
A	G	E	S	■	I	R	I	S	H
M	E	Y	E	R	■	A	N	N	A
■	■	■	A	A	A	■	L	O	U
J	E	R	R	Y	B	R	O	W	N
A	L	E	C	■	C	O	V	E	T
R	I	C	H	■	D	E	E	D	S

78

A	N	E	M	I	C	■	W	A	G
M	I	M	O	S	A	■	E	D	U
E	L	M	E	R	S	G	L	U	E
S	E	A	S	■	T	A	L	L	S
■	■	■	■	T	R	Y	S	T	S
H	O	H	O	H	O	■	■	■	■
E	F	I	L	E	■	P	I	E	R
F	U	D	D	Y	D	U	D	D	Y
T	S	E	■	R	E	N	E	G	E
Y	E	S	■	E	S	S	A	Y	S

79

R	E	S	T	E	D	■	A	P	P
I	C	E	A	G	E	■	R	I	O
T	H	E	M	O	N	K	E	E	S
Z	O	N	E	■	V	I	N	C	E
■	■	■	H	E	A	T	E	D	■
N	A	S	C	A	R	■	■	■	■
O	S	C	A	R	■	O	L	G	A
T	H	E	Y	A	N	K	E	E	S
M	E	N	■	S	T	R	E	E	P
E	S	T	■	S	H	A	R	K	S

80

P	A	B	L	O	■	A	L	A	S
O	R	I	O	N	■	N	I	L	E
S	M	A	L	L	V	I	L	L	E
S	A	L	■	Y	A	M	■	■	■
U	N	I	T	■	C	A	T	E	S
M	I	K	E	S	■	L	O	L	A
■	■	A	K	A	■	N	A	T	
T	H	E	B	I	G	C	I	T	Y
I	O	T	A	■	E	A	T	E	R
S	W	A	G	■	S	L	E	D	S

81

B	O	P	S	■	S	N	A	P	E
A	C	L	U	■	W	A	L	E	S
N	E	A	L	■	A	V	E	R	T
J	A	C	K	B	L	A	C	K	■
O	N	E	■	A	L	L	■	■	■
■	■	■	O	N	O	■	W	I	G
■	J	A	C	K	W	H	I	T	E
D	A	N	T	E	■	E	L	S	E
I	N	N	E	R	■	A	M	O	S
M	E	E	T	S	■	L	A	K	E

82

B	A	T	M	A	N	■	P	A	W
E	U	R	O	P	E	■	A	S	A
S	T	A	T	E	P	A	R	K	S
S	O	P	H	■	H	I	T	I	T
■	■	■	■	B	E	M	I	N	E
T	A	X	L	A	W	■	■	■	
O	N	R	E	D	■	L	O	S	E
S	K	A	T	E	P	A	R	K	S
S	H	Y	■	G	O	D	E	E	P
A	S	S	■	G	O	D	O	W	N

83

W	A	T	C	H	■	D	O	D	O
A	L	O	H	A	■	E	U	R	O
F	L	Y	I	N	G	F	I	S	H
F	R	I	■	S	H	E	■	■	
L	E	N	S	■	I	N	A	W	E
E	D	G	A	R	■	D	E	E	R
■	■	■	D	U	E	■	R	I	O
D	I	V	I	N	G	B	I	R	D
I	R	I	S	■	G	R	A	D	E
M	A	A	M	■	S	O	L	O	S

84

S	K	A	T	E	D	■	A	C	T
A	N	T	O	N	Y	■	M	O	E
G	O	O	G	L	E	M	A	P	S
E	X	P	O	■	J	A	N	E	T
■	■	■	G	O	E	A	S	Y	■
B	A	O	B	A	B	■	■	■	■
A	D	I	E	U	■	P	A	U	L
B	I	N	G	C	R	O	S	B	Y
A	O	K	■	H	U	N	T	E	R
R	S	S	■	E	E	Y	O	R	E

85

J	A	M	J	A	R	■	C	B	S
O	R	I	O	L	E	■	L	O	O
K	E	T	T	L	E	K	O	R	N
E	A	T	S	■	L	I	N	E	N
■	■	■	■	W	I	N	E	R	Y
S	T	J	O	H	N	■	■	■	■
A	R	E	N	A	'	S	T	E	P
C	A	T	T	L	E	C	A	L	L
K	I	T	■	E	L	A	P	S	E
S	T	A	■	R	I	N	S	E	D

86

H	O	T	E	L	S	■	F	O	E
I	N	A	B	I	T	■	L	I	L
T	I	M	B	E	R	W	O	L	F
F	O	P	■	S	A	O	■	■	■
O	N	E	S	■	P	O	L	O	S
R	Y	D	E	R	■	F	O	R	T
■	■	■	N	A	M	■	O	N	O
W	O	O	D	P	E	C	K	E	R
O	W	L	■	I	G	N	O	R	E
W	E	D	■	D	A	N	N	Y	S

87

H	I	G	H	■	A	D	O	P	T
A	C	E	D	■	L	E	P	E	R
L	I	T	T	L	E	L	U	L	U
A	L	I	V	E	■	I	S	E	E
S	Y	N	■	A	B	S	■	■	■
■	■	■	A	P	U	■	T	S	P
X	M	A	S	■	R	U	R	A	L
M	I	S	T	E	R	S	U	L	U
E	L	T	O	N	■	S	C	A	T
N	O	O	N	E	■	R	E	D	O

88

H	I	T	O	N	■	B	A	L	I
I	N	A	W	E	■	E	X	E	C
J	O	H	N	C	L	E	E	S	E
A	N	I	■	K	I	P	■	■	■
B	I	T	S	■	B	A	G	E	L
S	T	I	N	K	■	T	E	R	I
■	■	A	F	C	■	N	A	M	■
J	A	C	K	C	H	E	E	S	E
A	L	O	E	■	O	Y	V	E	Y
W	I	N	S	■	P	E	A	R	S

89

S	P	E	C	K	■	E	N	Y	A
W	A	Y	N	E	■	Q	U	I	P
I	R	E	N	E	D	U	N	N	E
V	A	L	■	P	O	I	■	■	■
E	D	I	T	■	S	T	R	I	P
L	E	D	I	N	■	Y	O	R	E
■	■	D	E	M	■	C	O	T	■
A	R	E	Y	O	U	D	O	N	E
H	U	L	U	■	N	I	C	E	R
A	T	O	P	■	I	P	O	D	S

90

H	I	R	T	■	A	N	D	U	P
A	Z	U	R	■	C	A	I	N	E
R	A	N	A	■	E	N	D	U	P
P	A	N	I	C	R	O	O	M	■
S	K	Y	L	A	B	■	■	■	■
■	■	■	B	I	A	N	C	A	■
■	S	O	N	I	C	B	O	O	M
N	I	X	O	N	■	D	O	R	A
A	L	E	V	E	■	U	S	E	S
W	O	N	A	T	■	L	E	S	S

91

C	D	S	■	F	I	R	S	T	S
H	E	W	■	I	S	A	I	A	H
A	J	A	■	G	L	I	T	Z	Y
S	A	Y	W	H	E	N	■	■	■
E	V	E	R	T	■	B	I	C	E
D	U	D	E	■	M	O	C	H	A
■	■	■	S	A	Y	W	H	A	T
S	E	E	T	H	E	■	B	I	O
A	N	T	L	E	R	■	I	S	U
M	O	D	E	M	S	■	N	E	T

92

```
S T I P E ■ H E M P
C O M I C ■ A L O E
H I T C H H I K E R
E L O ■ O A K ■ ■
M E L D ■ M U S T S
E D D I E ■ S H E A
■ ■ S K I ■ A N Y
G O I N G M Y W A Y
A N N E ■ D O N N E
D E N Y ■ B U S T S
```

93

```
B A S H ■ I D O L S
A N K A ■ S E P I A
S K I J U M P I N G
E L L I S ■ T E E S
D E L ■ A A H ■ ■
■ ■ K F C ■ A X E
A S T O ■ D O L E D
S K Y J A C K I N G
P E N A L ■ O B O E
S E E K S ■ K I N D
```

94

```
H A D I N ■ N I P S
O Z O N E ■ O A H U
B A C K G A M M O N
B L T ■ S L O ■ ■
L E O S ■ T R A M P
E A R T H ■ E L A L
■ ■ O A F ■ U S A
J A C K L E M M O N
F L O E ■ D O N N E
K I D S ■ S W I S S
```

95

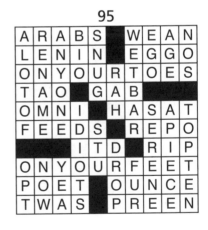

```
A R A B S ■ W E A N
L E N I N ■ E G G O
O N Y O U R T O E S
T A O ■ G A B ■ ■
O M N I ■ H A S A T
F E E D S ■ R E P O
■ ■ ■ I T D ■ R I P
O N Y O U R F E E T
P O E T ■ O U N C E
T W A S ■ P R E E N
```

A	A	A	■	S	T	I	F	F	S
L	I	T	■	K	I	L	L	I	T
I	S	T	H	I	S	L	O	V	E
A	L	I	B	I	■	S	P	E	W
S	E	C	O	N	D	■	■	■	■
■	■	■	G	E	H	R	I	G	
S	O	B	S	■	C	A	I	N	E
T	H	A	T	S	A	M	O	R	E
U	N	H	A	N	D	■	J	E	N
B	O	T	T	L	E	■	A	D	A

F	O	R	O	N	E	■	S	A	P
A	L	O	T	O	F	■	E	G	O
C	A	B	I	N	F	E	V	E	R
E	Y	E	S	■	E	V	E	N	T
■	■	■	S	C	E	N	T	S	
L	O	V	E	T	T	■	■	■	
A	N	E	A	R	■	A	R	G	O
I	T	S	T	O	O	C	O	L	D
R	A	P	■	B	I	L	L	E	D
S	P	A	■	E	L	U	D	E	S

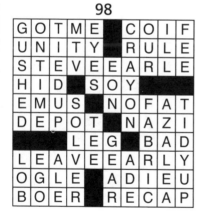

G	O	T	M	E	■	C	O	I	F
U	N	I	T	Y	■	R	U	L	E
S	T	E	V	E	E	A	R	L	E
H	I	D	■	S	O	Y	■		
E	M	U	S	■	N	O	F	A	T
D	E	P	O	T	■	N	A	Z	I
■	■	L	E	G	■	B	A	D	
L	E	A	V	E	E	A	R	L	Y
O	G	L	E	■	A	D	I	E	U
B	O	E	R	■	R	E	C	A	P

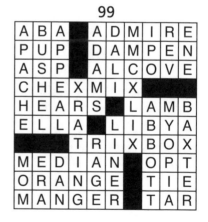

A	B	A	■	A	D	M	I	R	E
P	U	P	■	D	A	M	P	E	N
A	S	P	■	A	L	C	O	V	E
C	H	E	X	M	I	X	■	■	
H	E	A	R	S	■	L	A	M	B
E	L	L	A	■	L	I	B	Y	A
■	■	T	R	I	X	B	O	X	
M	E	D	I	A	N	■	O	P	T
O	R	A	N	G	E	■	T	I	E
M	A	N	G	E	R	■	T	A	R

104

105

106

107

108

L	O	T		L	A	M	E	N	T
O	R	E		A	D	A	G	I	O
G	I	N		L	A	M	O	N	T
J	O	N	H	A	M	M			
A	L	I	A	S		O	P	A	L
M	E	S	S		S	T	O	N	E
			I	M	A	H	O	G	G
B	A	N	D	I	T		B	E	G
E	L	A	I	N	E		A	L	E
D	A	N	C	E	D		H	A	D

109

B	A	S	H		F	E	L	I	X
A	R	O	D		E	V	I	T	E
M	I	N	T		B	A	S	E	S
B	E	A	V	E	R	D	A	M	
I	S	R		L	E	E			
			F	E	Z		I	D	S
	H	O	O	V	E	R	D	A	M
C	O	B	R	A		A	L	T	O
R	A	I	T	T		G	E	E	K
O	X	E	Y	E		E	D	D	Y

110

M	A	S	T		S	T	A	R	T
A	L	O	E		H	U	M	A	N
M	O	N	A		A	G	E	N	T
B	O	O	M	E	R	A	N	G	
O	F	F		A	P	T			
			F	R	I		K	O	S
	I	L	L	B	E	B	A	C	K
A	D	I	E	U		A	R	T	Y
B	L	E	E	D		J	E	E	P
S	E	U	S	S		A	N	T	E

111

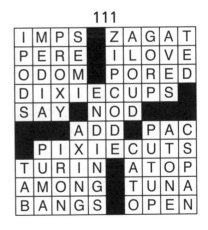

I	M	P	S		Z	A	G	A	T
P	E	R	E		I	L	O	V	E
O	D	O	M		P	O	R	E	D
D	I	X	I	E	C	U	P	S	
S	A	Y		N	O	D			
			A	D	D		P	A	C
	P	I	X	I	E	C	U	T	S
T	U	R	I	N		A	T	O	P
A	M	O	N	G		T	U	N	A
B	A	N	G	S		O	P	E	N

112

H	O	S	T	S	■	D	A	T	A
I	N	T	R	O	■	O	M	A	N
C	L	A	Y	M	A	T	I	O	N
K	I	N	■	E	V	E	■		
O	N	C	E	■	A	L	I	T	O
K	E	E	N	S	■	L	O	O	P
■			Z	A	P	■	D	Y	E
S	T	A	Y	C	A	T	I	O	N
P	A	L	M	■	D	A	N	T	E
A	X	L	E	■	S	P	E	A	R

113

S	E	R	B	■	C	O	L	O	R
I	G	O	R	■	A	W	A	K	E
R	O	Y	A	L	F	L	U	S	H
■			W	E	E	■	R	U	E
W	H	A	L	E	■	H	E	R	A
H	E	M	S	■	M	O	N	E	T
A	L	E	■	S	A	W	■		
T	E	N	T	H	P	L	A	C	E
I	N	D	I	E	■	E	B	A	Y
F	A	S	T	S	■	R	E	N	E

114

T	O	D	O	■	F	E	V	E	R
I	P	A	D	■	E	X	I	L	E
B	R	I	D	E	Z	I	L	L	A
B	A	L	S	A	■	S	E	A	L
S	H	Y	■	R	S	T	■		
■			S	P	A	■	C	T	R
S	W	A	P	■	N	E	H	R	U
L	I	V	I	N	G	R	O	O	M
A	F	I	R	E	■	R	S	V	P
B	I	D	E	D	■	S	E	E	S

115

M	A	C	■	R	E	J	E	C	T
O	L	E	■	O	R	A	L	L	Y
V	I	C	T	O	R	Y	L	A	P
E	V	I	L	S	■	Z	A	N	E
R	E	L	A	T	E	■			
■				S	M	O	K	E	S
T	W	I	G	■	I	R	A	Q	I
W	I	N	N	I	N	G	R	U	N
O	R	N	A	T	E	■	M	I	C
S	Y	S	T	E	M	■	A	P	E

116

117

P	E	A	K	■	J	A	M	I	N
O	G	L	E	■	O	B	A	M	A
P	O	L	Y	T	H	E	I	S	M
■	■	P	I	N	■	D	O	E	■
S	O	D	A	S	■	D	E	L	L
T	H	U	D	■	W	E	N	D	Y
A	S	P	■	B	I	B	■	■	■
M	U	L	T	I	G	R	A	I	N
P	R	E	E	N	■	I	D	L	E
S	E	X	E	S	■	S	O	L	O

S	C	A	R	■	B	A	R	O	N
H	U	L	U	■	A	M	O	U	R
I	R	O	N	■	Z	E	B	R	A
R	I	N	G	T	O	N	E	■	■
T	E	E	■	R	O	D	■	■	■
■	■	Y	A	K	■	H	E	M	■
■	R	I	G	A	T	O	N	I	■
A	L	I	K	E	■	A	P	E	X
T	I	M	E	D	■	M	E	M	E
M	E	S	S	Y	■	E	D	Y	S

118

B	O	G	S	■	F	I	N	C	H
A	C	R	E	■	O	B	A	M	A
M	E	A	L	■	X	E	N	O	N
B	A	D	M	I	N	T	O	N	■
I	N	S	A	N	E	■	■	■	■
■	■	■	A	W	A	R	D	S	■
■	G	O	O	D	S	P	O	R	T
P	A	D	U	A	■	A	S	I	A
B	L	I	T	Z	■	R	I	P	S
R	E	E	S	E	■	T	E	S	H

119

H	A	C	K	■	J	O	D	I	E
E	L	A	N	■	A	R	E	N	T
L	E	N	A	■	Y	E	A	R	S
P	R	O	V	O	L	O	N	E	■
S	T	E	E	L	E	■	■	■	■
■	■	■	I	N	A	S	E	C	■
■	P	R	O	V	O	U	T	A	H
S	A	U	D	I	■	R	A	G	E
A	N	N	I	E	■	A	L	L	S
P	E	T	E	R	■	S	E	E	S

120

A	L	E	S	■	V	I	A	L	S
M	O	R	E	■	A	S	S	E	T
O	K	I	E	■	N	A	I	V	E
K	I	C	K	M	E	■	D	E	W
■	■	T	E	S	T	E	R	S	
C	A	B	O	O	S	E	■	■	
E	R	A	■	W	A	S	H	M	E
D	E	N	I	M	■	L	A	U	D
A	T	A	R	I	■	A	L	I	G
R	O	L	E	X	■	S	O	R	E

121

S	C	O	T	S	■	O	D	I	N
A	R	R	O	W	■	B	O	S	E
S	A	M	O	A	■	G	R	E	W
S	T	A	N	D	B	Y	M	E	■
Y	E	N	■	D	E	N	■		
■	T	L	C	■	B	K	S		
H	A	V	E	A	S	E	A	T	
G	E	M	S	■	U	L	T	R	A
N	A	M	E	■	S	A	T	A	Y
P	L	O	T	■	E	V	E	N	S

122

S	O	B	S	■	S	L	O	P	S
P	H	E	W	■	N	E	H	R	U
A	B	L	E	■	O	N	I	O	N
D	O	L	L	Y	W	O	O	D	■
E	Y	E	L	I	D	■			
■	E	A	S	T	L	A			
B	O	L	L	Y	W	O	O	D	
R	O	W	E	D	■	A	M	I	D
A	R	E	N	T	■	M	E	R	E
P	E	S	T	O	■	P	I	E	R

123

C	H	A	S	M	■	B	A	C	K
R	O	G	U	E	■	A	L	A	N
Y	O	U	L	L	■	G	L	U	E
■	P	E	K	I	N	G	E	S	E
		S	A	Y	Y	E	S	■	
S	C	H	I	S	M	■			
L	H	A	S	A	A	P	S	O	
E	A	R	L	■	S	H	A	P	E
P	I	P	E	■	T	I	M	E	X
T	R	O	T	■	E	L	E	C	T

124

W	A	T	S	O	N	■	A	K	A
A	G	A	T	H	A	■	B	O	N
L	U	X	E	M	B	O	U	R	G
L	A	I	T	■	B	A	T	E	S
■	■	■	P	E	T	S	A	T	■
L	A	P	S	E	D	■	■	■	■
A	R	O	M	A	■	S	W	A	P
L	U	X	U	R	Y	C	A	R	S
A	B	E	■	L	E	A	V	E	S
W	A	S	■	S	A	N	E	S	T

125

B	E	T	A	■	J	A	D	E	D
T	R	I	M	■	O	L	I	V	E
W	R	E	A	K	H	A	V	O	C
■	■	■	Z	I	N	■	E	L	K
R	A	C	E	D	■	G	I	V	E
E	G	O	S	■	T	O	N	E	D
B	A	S	■	K	I	P	■	■	■
U	T	T	E	R	C	H	A	O	S
K	H	A	K	I	■	E	X	I	T
E	A	S	E	S	■	R	E	L	Y

126

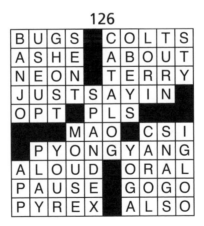

B	U	G	S	■	C	O	L	T	S
A	S	H	E	■	A	B	O	U	T
N	E	O	N	■	T	E	R	R	Y
J	U	S	T	S	A	Y	I	N	■
O	P	T	■	P	L	S	■	■	■
■	■	■	M	A	O	■	C	S	I
■	P	Y	O	N	G	Y	A	N	G
A	L	O	U	D	■	O	R	A	L
P	A	U	S	E	■	G	O	G	O
P	Y	R	E	X	■	A	L	S	O

127

L	E	A	K		T	W	I	S	T
B	A	R	E		R	A	N	T	O
J	U	M	P	F	O	R	J	O	Y
			T	U	T		U	N	O
D	I	D	I	N		F	R	E	T
I	R	O	N		D	O	E	S	A
S	A	D		P	A	L			
H	I	G	H	O	N	L	I	F	E
U	S	E	U	P		O	P	A	L
P	E	S	T	S		W	O	R	M

128

Y	A	K	S		B	A	N	T	U
A	B	E	T		U	S	U	R	P
C	H	A	I		T	I	M	E	S
H	O	N	E	S	T	A	B	E	
T	R	U	S	T	S				
				R	I	S	I	N	G
	S	I	L	E	N	T	C	A	L
C	U	R	I	E		A	I	D	E
A	L	O	F	T		V	E	I	N
B	U	N	T	S		E	R	R	S